TRUE RICHES

OR, WEALTH WITHOUT WINGS

T. S. ARTHUR

1st WORLD
LIBRARY
Literary Society

True Riches

T. S. Arthur

© 1st World Library, 2006
PO Box 2211
Fairfield, IA 52556
www.1stworldlibrary.com
First Edition

LCCN: 2006907731

Softcover ISBN: 1-4218-2455-8
Hardcover ISBN: 1-4218-2355-1
eBook ISBN: 1-4218-2555-4

Purchase *"True Riches"*
as a traditional bound book at:
www.1stWorldLibrary.com/purchase.asp?ISBN=1-4218-2455-8

1st World Library is a literary, educational organization
dedicated to:

- Creating a free internet library of downloadable ebooks

- Hosting writing competitions and offering book
publishing scholarships.

Interested in more 1st World Library books?
contact: literacy@1stworldlibrary.com
Check us out at: www.1stworldlibrary.com

1st World Library Literary Society

Giving Back to the World

"If you want to work on the core problem, it's early school literacy."

- James Barksdale, former CEO of Netscape

"No skill is more crucial to the future of a child, or to a democratic and prosperous society, than literacy."

- Los Angeles Times

Literacy... means far more than learning how to read and write... The aim is to transmit... knowledge and promote social participation."

- UNESCO

"Literacy is not a luxury, it is a right and a responsibility. If our world is to meet the challenges of the twenty-first century we must harness the energy and creativity of all our citizens."

- President Bill Clinton

"Parents should be encouraged to read to their children, and teachers should be equipped with all available techniques for teaching literacy, so the varying needs and capacities of individual kids can be taken into account."

- Hugh Mackay

INTRODUCTION

The original title chosen for this book was "Riches without Wings;" but the author becoming aware, before giving it a permanent form, that a volume bearing a similar title had appeared some years ago, of which a new edition was about to be issued, thought it best to substitute therefor, "True Riches; or, Wealth without Wings," which, in fact, expresses more accurately the character and scope of his story.

The lessons herein taught are such as cannot be learned too early, nor dwelt on too long or too often, by those who are engaged in the active and all-absorbing duties of life. In the struggle for natural riches - the wealth that meets the eye and charms the imagination – how many forget that *true* riches can *only* be laid up in the heart; and that, without these true riches, which have no wings, gold, the god of this world, cannot bestow a single blessing! To give this truth a varied charm for young and old, the author has made of it a new presentation, and, in so doing, sought to invest it with all the winning attractions in his power to bestow.

To parents who regard the best interests of their children, and to young men and women just stepping upon the world's broad stage of action, we offer our book, in the confident belief that it contains vital principles, which, if laid up in the mind, will, like good seed in good ground, produce an after-harvest, in the garnering of which there will be great joy.

CHAPTER I

"A fair day's business. A *very* fair day's business," said Leonard Jasper, as he closed a small account-book, over which he had been poring, pencil in hand, for some ten minutes. The tone in which he spoke expressed more than ordinary gratification.

"To what do the sales amount?" asked a young man, clerk to the dealer, approaching his principal as he spoke.

"To just two hundred dollars, Edward. It's the best day we've had for a month."

"The best, in more than one sense," remarked the young man, with a meaning expression.

"You're right there, too," said Jasper, with animation, rubbing his hands together as he spoke, in the manner of one who is particularly well pleased with himself. "I made two or three trades that told largely on the sunny side of profit and loss account."

"True enough. Though I've been afraid, ever since you sold that piece of velvet to Harland's wife, that you cut rather deeper than was prudent."

"Not a bit of it - not a bit of it! Had I asked her three dollars a yard, she would have wanted it for two. So I said six, to begin with, expecting to fall extensively; and, to put a good face on the matter, told her that it cost within a fraction of what I asked to make the importation - remarking, at the same time, that the goods were too rich in quality to bear a profit, and were only kept as a matter of accommodation to certain customers."

"And she bought at five?"

"Yes; thinking she had obtained the velvet at seventy-five cents a yard less than its cost. Generous customer, truly!"

"While you, in reality, made two dollars and a half on every yard she bought."

"Precisely that sum."

"She had six yards."

"Yes; out of which we made a clear profit of fifteen dollars. That will do, I'm thinking. Operations like this count up fast."

"Very fast. But, Mr. Jasper" -

"But what, Edward?"

"Is it altogether prudent to multiply operations of this character? Won't it make for you a bad reputation, and thus diminish, instead of increasing, your custom?"

"I fear nothing of the kind. One-half the people are not satisfied unless you cheat them. I've handled the yardstick, off and on, for the last fifteen or twenty years, and I think my observation during that time is worth something. It tells me this - that a bold face, a smooth tongue, and an easy conscience are worth more in our business than any other qualities. With these you may do as you list. They tell far better than all the 'one-price' and fair-dealing professions, in which people have little faith. In fact, the mass will overreach if they can, and therefore regard these 'honest' assumptions with suspicion."

The young man, Edward Claire, did not make a reply for nearly a minute. Something in the words of Mr. Jasper had fixed his thought, and left him, for a brief space of time, absorbed in his own reflections.

Lifting, at length, his eyes, which had been resting on the floor, he said -

"Our profit on to-day's sales must reach very nearly fifty dollars."

"Just that sum, if I have made a right estimate," replied Jasper; "and that is what I call a fair day's business."

While he was yet speaking, a lad entered the store, and laid upon the counter a small sealed package, bearing the superscription, "Leonard Jasper, Esq." The merchant cut the red tape with which it was tied, broke the seal, and opening the package, took therefrom several papers, over which he ran his eyes hurriedly; his clerk, as he did so, turning away.

"What's this?" muttered Jasper to himself, not at first clearly comprehending the nature of the business to which the communication related. "Executor! To what? Oh! ah! Estate of Ruben Elder. Humph! What possessed him to trouble me with this business? I've no time to play executor to an estate, the whole proceeds of which would hardly fill my trousers' pocket. He was a thriftless fellow at best, and never could more than keep his head out of water. His debts will swallow up every thing, of course, saving my commissions, which I would gladly throw in to be rid of this business."

With this, Jasper tossed the papers into his desk, and, taking up his hat, said to his clerk - "You may shut the store, Edward. Before you leave, see that every thing is made safe."

The merchant than retired, and wended his way homeward.

Edward Claire seemed in no hurry to follow this example. His first act was to close the window-shutters and door - turning the key in the latter, and remaining inside.

Entirely alone, and hidden from observation, the young man seated himself, and let his thoughts, which seemed to be active on some subject, take their own way. He was soon entirely absorbed. Whatever were his thoughts, one thing would have been apparent to an observer - they did not run in a quiet stream. Something disturbed their current, for his brow was knit, his compressed lips had a disturbed motion, and his hands moved about at times uneasily. At length he arose, not hurriedly, but with a deliberate motion, threw his arms behind him, and, bending forward, with his eyes cast down, paced the length of the store two or three times, backward and forward, slowly.

"Fifty dollars profit in one day," he at length said, half audibly. "That will do, certainly. I'd be contented with a tenth part of the sum. He's bound to get rich; that's plain. Fifty dollars in a single day! Leonard Jasper, you're a shrewd one. I shall have to lay aside some of my old-fashioned squeamishness, and take a few lessons from so accomplished a teacher. But, he's a downright cheat!"

Some better thought had swept suddenly, in a gleam of light, across the young man's mind, showing him the true nature of the principles from which the merchant acted, and, for the moment, causing his whole nature to revolt against them. But the light faded slowly; a state of darkness and confusion followed, and then the old current of thought moved on as before.

Slowly, and now with an attitude of deeper abstraction, moved the young man backward and forward the entire length of the room, of which he was the sole occupant. He *felt* that he was alone, that no human eye could note a single movement. Of the all-seeing Eye he thought not - his spirit's evil counsellors, drawn intimately nigh to him through inclinations to evil, kept that consciousness from his mind.

T. S. Arthur

At length Claire turned to the desk upon which were the account-books that had been used during the day, and commenced turning the leaves of one of them in a way that showed only a half-formed purpose. There was an impulse to something in his mind; an impulse not yet expressed in any form of thought, though in the progress toward something definite.

"Fifty dollars a day!" he murmurs. Ah, that shows the direction of his mind. He is still struggling in temptation, and with all his inherited cupidities bearing him downward.

Suddenly he starts, turns his head, and listens eagerly, and with a strange agitation. Some one had tried the door. For a few moments he stood in an attitude of the most profound attention. But the trial was not repeated. How audibly, to his own ears, throbbed his heart! How oppressed was his bosom! How, in a current of fire, rushed the blood to his over-excited brain!

The hand upon the door was but an ordinary occurrence. It might now be only a customer, who, seeing a light within, hoped to supply some neglected want, or a friend passing by, who wished for a few words of pleasant gossip. At any other time Claire would have stepped quickly and with undisturbed expectation to receive the applicant for admission. But guilty thoughts awakened their nervous attendants, suspicion and fear, and these had sounded an instant alarm.

Still, very still, sat Edward Claire, even to the occasional suppression of his breathing, which, to him, seemed strangely loud.

Several minutes elapsed, and then the young man commenced silently to remove the various account-books to their nightly safe deposit in the fire-proof. The cash-box, over the contents of which he lingered, counting note by note and coin by coin, several times repeated, next took its place with the books. The heavy iron door swung to, the key traversed noiselessly the delicate and complicated wards, was removed and deposited in a place of safety; and, yet unrecovered from his mood of abstraction, the clerk left the store, and took his way homeward. From that hour Edward Claire was to be the subject of a fierce temptation. He had admitted an evil suggestion, and had warmed it in the earth of his mind, even to germination. Already a delicate root had penetrated the soil, and was extracting food therefrom. Oh! Why did he not instantly pluck it out, when the hand of an infant would have sufficed in strength for the task? Why did he let it remain, shielding it from the cold winds of rational truth and the hot sun of good affections, until it could live, sustained by its own organs of appropriation and nutrition? Why did he let it remain until its lusty growth gave sad promise of an evil tree, in which birds of night find shelter and build nests for their young?

Let us introduce another scene and another personage, who will claim, to some extent, the reader's attention.

There were two small but neatly, though plainly, furnished rooms, in the second story of a house located in a retired street. In one of these rooms tea was prepared, and near the tea-table sat a young woman, with a sleeping babe nestled to her bosom. She was fair-faced and sunny-haired; and in her blue eyes lay, in calm beauty, sweet tokens of a pure and loving heart. How tenderly she looked down, now and then, upon the slumbering cherub whose winning ways and murmurs of affection had blessed her through the day! Happy young wife! these are thy halcyon days. Care has not thrown upon thee a single shadow from his gloomy wing, and hope pictures the smiling future with a sky of sunny brightness.

"How long he stays away!" had just passed her lips, when the sound of well-known footsteps was heard in the passage below. A brief time, and then the room-door opened, and Edward Claire came in. What a depth of tenderness was in his voice as he bent his lips to those of his young wife, murmuring -

"My Edith!" and then touching, with a gentler pressure, the white forehead of his sleeping babe.

"You were late this evening, dear," said Edith, looking into the face of her husband, whose eyes drooped under her earnest gaze.

"Yes," he replied, with a slight evasion in his tone and manner; "we have been busier than usual to-day."

As he spoke the young wife arose, and taking her slumbering child into the adjoining chamber, laid it gently in its crib. Then returning, she made the tea - the kettle stood boiling by the grate - and in a little while they sat down to their evening meal.

Edith soon observed that her husband was more thoughtful and less talkative than usual. She asked, however, no direct question touching this change; but regarded what he did say with closer attention, hoping to draw a correct inference, without seeming to notice his altered mood.

"Mr. Jasper's business is increasing?" she said, somewhat interrogatively, while they still sat at the table, an expression of her husband's leading to this remark.

"Yes, increasing very rapidly," replied Claire, with animation. "The fact is, he is going to get rich. Do you know that his profit on to-day's sales amounted to fifty dollars?"

"So much?" said Edith, yet in a tone that showed no surprise or particular interest in the matter.

"Fifty dollars a day," resumed Claire, "counting three hundred week-days in the year, gives the handsome sum of fifteen thousand dollars in the year. I'd be satisfied with as much in five years."

There was more feeling in the tone of his voice than he had

meant to betray. His young wife lifted her eyes to his face, and looked at him with a wonder she could not conceal.

"Contentment, dear," said she, in a gentle, subdued, yet tender voice, "is great gain. We have enough, and more than enough, to make us happy. Natural riches have no power to fill the heart's most yearning affections; and how often do they take to themselves wings and fly away."

"Enough, dear!" replied Edward Claire, smiling. "O no, not enough, by any means. Five hundred dollars a year is but a meagre sum. What does it procure for us? Only these two rooms and the commonest necessaries of life. We cannot even afford the constant service of a domestic."

"Why, Edward! what has come over you? Have I complained?"

"No, dear, no. But think you I have no ambition to see my wife take a higher place than this?"

"Ambition! Do not again use that word," said Edith, very earnestly. "What has love to do with ambition? What have we to do with the world and its higher places? Will a more elegant home secure for us a purer joy than we have known and still know in this our Eden? Oh, my husband! do not let such thoughts come into your mind. Let us be content with what God in his wisdom provides, assured that it is best for us. In envying the good of another, we destroy our own good. There is a higher wealth than gold, Edward; and it supplies higher wants. There are riches without wings; they lie scattered about our feet; we may fill our coffers, if we will. Treasures of good affections and true thoughts are worth more than all earthly riches, and will bear us far more safely and happily through the world; such treasures are given to all who will receive them, and given in lavish abundance. Let us secure of this wealth, Edward, a liberal share."

"Mere treasures of the mind, Edith, do not sustain natural life, do not supply natural demands. They build no houses; they

T. S. Arthur

provide not for increasing wants. We cannot always remain in the ideal world; the sober realities of life will drag us down."

The simple-hearted, true-minded young wife was not understood by her husband. She felt this, and felt it oppressively.

"Have we not enough, Edward, to meet every real want?" she urged. "Do we desire better food or better clothing? Would our bodies be more comfortable because our carpets were of richer material, and our rooms filled with costlier furniture? O no! If not contented with such things as Providence gives us to-day, we shall not find contentment in what he gives us to-morrow; for the same dissatisfied heart will beat in our bosoms. Let Mr. Jasper get rich, if he can; we will not envy his possessions."

"I do not envy him, Edith," replied Claire. "But I cannot feel satisfied with the small salary he pays me. My services are, I know, of greater value than he estimates them, and I feel that I am dealt by unjustly."

Edith made no answer. The subject was repugnant to her feelings, and she did not wish to prolong it. Claire already regretted its introduction. So there was silence for nearly a minute.

When the conversation flowed on again, it embraced a different theme, but had in it no warmth of feeling. Not since they had joined hands at the altar, nearly two years before, had they passed so embarrassed and really unhappy an evening as this. A tempting spirit had found its way into their Paradise, burning with a fierce desire to mar its beauty.

CHAPTER II

"Oh, what a dream I have had!" exclaimed Mrs. Claire, starting suddenly from sleep, just as the light began to come in dimly through the windows on the next morning; and, as she spoke, she caught hold of her husband, and clung to him, frightened and trembling.

"Oh, such a dream!" she added, as her mind grew clearer, and she felt better assured of the reality that existed. "I thought, love, that we were sitting in our room, as we sit every evening - baby asleep, I sewing, and you, as usual, reading aloud. How happy we were! happier, it seemed, than we had ever been before. A sudden loud knock startled us both. Then two men entered, one of whom drew a paper from his pocket, declaring, as he did so, that you were arrested at the instance of Mr. Jasper, who accused you with having robbed him of a large amount of money."

"Why, Edith!" ejaculated Edward Claire, in a voice of painful surprise. He, too, had been dreaming, and in his dream he had done what his heart prompted him to do on the previous evening - to act unfaithfully toward his employer.

"Oh, it was dreadful! dreadful!" continued Edith. "Rudely they seized and bore you away. Then came the trial. Oh, I see it all as plainly as if it had been real. You, my good, true, noble-hearted husband, who had never wronged another, even in thought - you were accused of robbery in the presence of hundreds, and positive witnesses were brought forward to

T. S. Arthur

prove the terrible charge. All they alleged was believed by those who heard. The judges pronounced you guilty, and then sentenced you to a gloomy prison. They were bearing you off, when, in my agony, I awoke. It was terrible, terrible! yet, thank God! only a dream, a fearful dream!"

Claire drew his arms around his young wife, and clasped her with a straining embrace to his bosom. He made no answer for some time. The relation of a dream so singular, under the circumstances, had startled him, and he almost feared to trust his voice in response. At length, with a deeply-drawn, sighing breath, nature's spontaneous struggle for relief, he said -

"Yes, dear, that was a fearful dream. The thought of it makes me shudder. But, after all, it was only a dream; the whispering of a malignant spirit in your ear. Happily, his power to harm extends no further. The fancy may be possessed in sleep, but the reason lies inactive, and the hands remain idle. No guilt can stain the spirit. The night passes, and we go abroad in the morning as pure as when we laid our heads wearily to rest."

"And more," added Edith, her mind fast recovering itself; "with a clearer perception of what is true and good. The soul's disturbed balance finds its equilibrium. It is not the body alone that is refreshed and strengthened. The spirit, plied with temptation after temptation through the day, and almost ready to yield when the night cometh, finds rest also, and time to recover its strength. In the morning it goes forth again, stronger for its season of repose. How often, as the day dawned, have I lifted my heart and thanked God for sleep!"

Thus prompted, an emotion of thankfulness arose in the breast of Claire, but the utterance was kept back from the lips. He had a secret, a painful and revolting secret, in his heart, and he feared lest something should betray its existence to his wife. What would he not have given at the moment to have blotted out for ever the memory of thoughts too earnestly cherished on the evening before, when he was alone with the tempter?

There was a shadow on the heart of Edith Claire. The unusual mood of her husband on the previous evening, and the dream which had haunted her through the night, left impressions that could not be shaken off. She had an instinct of danger - danger lurking in the path of one in whom her very life was bound up.

When Edward was about leaving her to go forth for the day, she lingered by his side and clung to him, as if she could not let him pass from the safe shelter of home.

"Ah! if I could always be with you!" said Edith - "if we could ever move on, hand in hand and side by side, how full to running over would be my cup of happiness!"

"Are we not ever side by side, dear?" replied Claire, tenderly. "You are present to my thought all the day."

"And you to mine. O yes! yes! We *are* moving side by side; our mutual thought gives presence. Yet it was the bodily presence I desired. But that cannot be."

"Good-bye, love! Good-bye, sweet one!" said Claire, kissing his wife, and gently pressing his lips upon those of the babe she held in her arms. He then passed forth, and took his way to the store of Leonard Jasper, in whose service he had been for two years, or since the date of his marriage.

A scene transpired a few days previous to this, which we will briefly describe. Three persons were alone in a chamber, the furniture of which, though neither elegant nor costly, evinced taste and refinement. Lying upon a bed was a man, evidently near the time of his departure from earth. By his side, and bending over him, was a woman almost as pale as himself. A little girl, not above five years of age, sat on the foot of the bed, with her eyes fixed on the countenance of her father, for such was the relation borne to her by the sick man. A lovely creature she was - beautiful even beyond the common beauty of childhood. For a time a solemn stillness reigned through the chamber. A few low-spoken words had passed between the parents of the child, and then, for a brief period, all was deep, oppressive silence. This was interrupted, at length, by the mother's unrestrained sobs, as she laid her face upon the bosom of her husband, so soon to be taken from her, and wept aloud.

No word of remonstrance or comfort came from the sick man's lips. He only drew his arm about the weeper's neck, and held her closer to his heart.

The troubled waters soon ran clear: there was calmness in their depths.

"It is but for a little while, Fanny," said he, in a feeble yet steady voice; "only for a little while."

"I know; I feel that here," was replied, as a thin, white hand was laid against the speaker's bosom. "And I could patiently await my time, but" -

Her eyes glanced yearningly toward the child, who sat gazing upon her parents, with an instinct of approaching evil at her heart.

Too well did the dying man comprehend the meaning of this glance.

"God will take care of her. He will raise her up friends," said he quickly; yet, even as he spoke, his heart failed him.

"All that is left to us is our trust in Him," murmured the wife and mother. Her voice, though so low as to be almost a whisper, was firm. She realized, as she spoke, how much of bitterness was in the parting hours of the dying one, and she felt that duty required her to sustain him, so far as she had the strength to do so. And so she nerved her woman's heart, almost breaking as it was, to bear and hide her own sorrows, while she strove to comfort and strengthen the failing spirit of her husband.

"God is good," said she, after a brief silence, during which she was striving for the mastery over her weakness. As she spoke, she leaned over the sick man, and looked at him lovingly, and with the smile of an angel on her countenance.

"Yes, God is good, Fanny. Have we not proved this, again and again?" was returned, a feeble light coming into the speaker's pale face.

"A thousand times, dear! a thousand times!" said the wife, earnestly. "He is infinite in his goodness, and we are his children."

"Yes, his children," was the whispered response. And over and over again he repeated the words, "His children;" his voice falling lower and lower each time, until at length his eyes closed, and his in-going thought found no longer an utterance.

Twilight had come. The deepening shadows were fast obscuring all objects in the sick-chamber, where silence reigned, profound almost as death.

"He sleeps," whispered the wife, as she softly raised herself from her reclining position on the bed. "And dear Fanny sleeps also," was added, as her eyes rested upon the unconscious form of her child.

Two hours later, and the last record was made in Ruben Elder's Book of Life.

For half an hour before the closing scene, his mind was clear, and he then spoke calmly of what he had done for those who were to remain behind.

"To Leonard Jasper, my old friend," said he to his wife, "I have left the management of my affairs. He will see that every thing is done for the best. There is not much property, yet enough to insure a small income; and, when you follow me to the better land, sufficient for the support and education of our child."

T. S. Arthur

Peacefully, after this, he sank away, and, like a weary child falling into slumber, slept that sleep from which the awakening is in another world.

How Leonard Jasper received the announcement of his executorship has been seen. The dying man had referred to him as an old friend; but, as the reader has already concluded, there was little room in his sordid heart for so pure a sentiment as that of friendship. He, however, lost no time in ascertaining the amount of property left by Elder, which consisted of two small houses in the city, and a barren tract of about sixty acres of land, somewhere in Pennsylvania, which had been taken for a debt of five hundred dollars. In view of his death, Elder had wound up his business some months before, paid off what he owed, and collected in nearly all outstanding accounts; so that little work remained for his executor, except to dispose of the unprofitable tract of land and invest the proceeds.

On the day following the opening of our story, Jasper, who still felt annoyed at the prospect of more trouble than profit in the matter of his executorship, made a formal call upon the widow of his old friend.

The servant, to whom he gave his name, stated that Mrs. Elder was so ill as not to be able to leave her room.

"I will call again, then, in a few days," said he. "Be sure you give her my name correctly. Mr. Jasper - Leonard Jasper."

The face of the servant wore a troubled aspect.

"She is very sick, sir," said she, in a worried, hesitating manner. "Won't you take a seat, for a moment, until I go up and tell her that you are here? Maybe she would like to see you. I think I heard her mention your name a little while ago."

Jasper sat down, and the domestic left the room. She was gone but a short time, when she returned and said that Mrs. Elder wished to see him. Jasper arose and followed her up-stairs.

There were some strange misgivings in his heart - some vague, troubled anticipations, that oppressed his feelings. But he had little time for thought ere he was ushered into the chamber of his friend's widow.

A single glance sufficed to tell him the whole sad truth of the case. There was no room for mistake. The bright, glazed eyes, the rigid, colourless lips, the ashen countenance, all testified that the hour of her departure drew nigh. How strong, we had almost said, how beautiful, was the contrasted form and features of her lovely child, whose face, so full of life and rosy health, pressed the same pillow that supported her weary head.

Feebly the dying woman extended her hand, as Mr. Jasper came in, saying, as she did so -

"I am glad you have come; I was about sending for you."

A slight tremor of the lips accompanied her words, and it was plain that the presence of Jasper, whose relation to her and her child she understood, caused a wave of emotion to sweep over her heart.

"I am sorry, Mrs. Elder, to find you so very ill," said Jasper, with as much of sympathy in his voice as he could command. "Has your physician been here to-day?"

"It is past that, sir - past that," was replied. "There is no further any hope for me in the physician's art."

A sob choked all further utterance.

How oppressed was the cold-hearted, selfish man of the world! His thoughts were all clouded, and his lips for a time sealed. As the dying woman said, so he felt that it was. The time of her departure had come. An instinct of self-protection - protection for his feelings - caused him, after a few moments, to say, and he turned partly from the bed as he spoke -

T. S. Arthur

"Some of your friends should be with you, madam, at this time. Let me go for them. Have you a sister or near relative in the city?"

The words and movement of Mr. Jasper restored at once the conscious self-possession of the dying mother, and she raised herself partly up with a quick motion, and a gleam of light in her countenance.

"Oh, sir," she said eagerly, "do not go yet. I have no sister, no near relative; none but you to whom I can speak my last words and give my last injunction. You were my husband's friend while he lived, and to you has he committed the care of his widow and orphan. I am called, alas, too soon! to follow him; and now, in the sight of God, and in the presence of his spirit - for I feel that he is near us now - I commit to you the care of this dear child. Oh, sir! be to her as a father. Love her tenderly, and care for her as if she were your own. Her heart is rich with affection, and upon you will its treasures be poured out. Take her! take her as your own! Here I give to you, in this the solemn hour of my departure, that which to me is above all price."

And as she said this, with a suddenly renewed strength, she lifted the child, and, ere Jasper could check the movement, placed her in his arms. Then, with one long, eager, clinging kiss pressed upon the lips of that child, she sank backward on the bed; and life, which had flashed up brightly for a moment, went out in this world for ever.

CHAPTER III

Leonard Jasper would have been less than human had he borne such an assault upon his feelings without emotion; less than human had his heart instantly and spontaneously rejected the dying mother's wildly eloquent appeal. He was bewildered, startled, even deeply moved.

The moment he could, with propriety and a decent regard for appearances, get away from the house where he had witnessed so painful a scene, he returned to his place of business in a sobered, thoughtful state of mind. He had not anticipated so direct a guardianship of Ruben Elder's child as it was evident would now devolve upon him, in consequence of the mother's death. Here was to be trouble for him - this was his feeling so soon as there was a little time for reaction - and trouble without profit. He would have to take upon himself the direct charge of the little girl, and duly provide for her maintenance and education.

"If there is property enough for this, well and good," he muttered to himself; he had not yet become acquainted with the real state of affairs. "If not," he added, firmly, "the loss will be hers; that is all. I shall have sufficient trouble and annoyance, without being put to expense."

For some time after his return to his store, Jasper refrained from entering upon any business. During at least fifteen or twenty minutes, he sat at his desk, completely absorbed in thought. At length he called to Edward Claire, his principal

T. S. Arthur

clerk, and said that he wished to speak a few words with him. The young man came back from the counter to where he was sitting, wondering what had produced the very apparent change in his employer's state of mind.

"Edward," said Mr. Jasper, in a low, serious voice, "there is a little matter that I must get you to attend to for me. It is not very pleasant, it is true; though nothing more than people are required to do every day. You remember Mr. Elder, Ruben Elder, who formerly kept store in Second street?"

"Very well."

"He died last week."

"I noticed his death in the papers."

"He has appointed me his executor."

"Ah?"

"Yes; and I wish to my heart he had appointed somebody else. I've too much business of my own to attend to."

"Of course," said Claire, "you will receive your regular commissions for attending to the settlement of his estate."

"Poor picking there," replied Jasper, shrugging his shoulders. "I'd very cheerfully give up the profit to be rid of the trouble. But that doesn't signify now. Elder has left his affairs in my hands, and I must give them at least some attention. I'm not coming to the point, however. A little while ago I witnessed the most painful scene that ever fell under my eyes."

"Ah!"

"Yes, truly. Ugh! It makes the chills creep over me as I think of it. Last evening I received regular notification of my appoint-ment as executor to Elder's estate, and to-day thought it only right to call upon the widow, and see if any present service were needed by the family. Such a scene as I encountered! Mrs. Elder was just at the point of death, and expired a few moments after my entrance. Besides a single domestic and a child, I was the only witness of her last extremity."

"Shocking!"

"You may well say shocking, Edward, unprepared as I was for such an occurrence. My nerves are quivering yet."

"Then the widow is dead also?"

"Yes; both have gone to their long home."

"How many children are left?"

"Only one - a little girl, not, I should think, above four years of age."

"Some near relative will, I presume, take charge of her."

"In dying, the mother declared that she had no friend to whom she could leave the child. On me, therefore, devolves the care of seeing to its maintenance."

"No friend. Poor child! and of so tender an age!"

"She is young, certainly, to be left alone in the world."

Jasper uttered these words, but felt nothing of the sad meaning they involved.

"What disposition will you make of her?" asked Claire.

"I've had no time to think of that yet. Other matters are first to be regarded. So let me come to the point. Mrs. Elder is dead; and, as far as I could see, there is no living soul, beyond a frightened servant, to do any thing. Whether she will have the presence of mind to call in the neighbours, is more than I can say. I left in the bewilderment of the moment; and now remember me that something is to be done for the dead. Will you go to the house, and see what is needed? In the next block is an undertaker; you had better call, on your way, and ask him to go with you. All arrangements necessary for the funeral can be left in his hands. Just take this whole matter off of me, Edward, and I will be greatly obliged to you. I have a good many things on my mind, that must receive close attention."

The young man offered no objection, although the service was far from being agreeable. On his return, after the absence of an hour, Jasper had, of course, many inquiries to make. Claire appeared serious. The fact was, he had seen enough to touch his feelings deeply. The grief of the orphaned child, as he was a witness thereto, had brought tears upon his cheeks, in spite of every manly effort to restrain them. Her extreme beauty struck him at the first glance, even obscured as it was under a vail of sorrow and weeping.

"There were several persons in, you say?" remarked Jasper, after Claire had related a number of particulars.

"Yes, three or four."

"Ladies, of course?"

"Yes."

"Did any of them propose to take the child home with them?"

"Not directly. One woman asked me a number of questions about the little girl."

"Of what nature?"

"As to whether there were any relatives or particular friends who would take charge of her?"

"And you told her there were none?"

"Yes; none of whom I had any knowledge."

"Well? What had she to say to that?"

"She wanted to know if there would be any thing for the child's support. I said that there would, in all probability."

"Well?"

"Then she gave me to understand, that if no one took the child, she might be induced to board her for a while, until other arrangements were made."

"Did you give her to understand that this was practicable?"

"No, sir."

"Why not? She will have to be boarded, you know."

"I neither liked the woman's face, manner, nor appearance."

"Why not?"

"Oh, she was a vulgar, coarse, hard-looking creature to my eyes."

"Kind hearts often lie concealed under unpromising externals."

"True; but they lie not concealed under that exterior, be well assured, Mr. Jasper. No, no. The child who has met with so sad a loss as that of a mother, needs the tenderest guardianship. At best, the case is hard enough."

Jasper did not respond to this humane sentiment, for there was no pity in him. The waves of feeling, stirred so suddenly a few hours before, had all subsided, and the surface of his heart bore no ripple of emotion. He thought not of the child as an object

T. S. Arthur

claiming his regard, but as a trouble and a hinderance thrown in his way, to be disposed of as summarily as possible.

"I'm obliged to you, Edward, for the trouble you have taken in my stead," he remarked, after a slight pause. "To-morrow, I may wish you to call there again. Of course, the neighbours will give needful attention until the funeral takes place. By that time, perhaps, the child will have made a friend of some one of them, and secure, through this means, a home for the present. It is, for us, a troublesome business at best, though it will soon be over."

A person coming in at the moment, Claire left his employer to attend at the counter. The new customer, it was quickly perceived by the clerk, was one who might readily be deceived into buying the articles for which she inquired, at a rate far in advance of their real value; and he felt instantly tempted to ask her a very high price. Readily, for it was but acting from habit, did he yield to this temptation. His success was equal to his wishes. The woman, altogether unsuspicious of the cheat practised upon her, paid for her purchases the sum of ten dollars above their true value. She lingered a short time after settling her bill, and made some observation upon a current topic of the day. One or two casually-uttered sentiments did not fall like refreshing dew upon the feelings of Claire, but rather stung him like words of sharp rebuke, and made him half regret the wrong he had done to her. He felt relieved when she retired.

It so happened that, while this customer was in, Jasper left the store. Soon after, a clerk went to dinner. Only a lad remained with Claire, and he was sent up-stairs to arrange some goods.

The hour of temptation had again come, and the young man's mind was overshadowed by the powers of darkness.

"Ten dollars clear gain on that transaction," said he to himself, as he drew open the money-drawer in which he had deposited the cash paid to him by his late customer.

For some time his thoughts were busy, while his fingers toyed with the gold and bills in the drawer. Two five-dollar pieces were included in the payment just received.

"Jasper, surely, ought to be satisfied with one of these." Thus he began to argue with himself. "I drove the bargain; am I not entitled to a fair proportion of the profit? It strikes me so. What wrong will it be to him? Wrong? Humph! Wrong? The wrong has been done already; but it falls not on his head.

"If I am to do this kind of work for him," - the feelings of Claire now commenced running in a more disturbed channel; there were deep contractions on his forehead, and his lips were shut firmly, - "this kind of work, I must have a share of the benefit. If I am to sell my soul, Leonard Jasper shall not have the whole price."

Deliberately, as he spoke this within himself, did Claire take from the drawer a five-dollar gold piece, and thrust it into his pocket.

"Mine, not his," were the words with which he approved the act. At the same instant Jasper entered. The young man's heart gave a sudden bound, and there was guilt in his face, but Jasper did not read its true expression.

"Well, Edward," said he, cheerfully, "what luck did you have with the old lady? Did she make a pretty fair bill?"

"So-so," returned Claire, with affected indifference; "about thirty dollars."

"Ah! so much?"

"Yes; and, what is better, I made her pay pretty strong. She was from the country."

"That'll do." And Jasper rubbed his hands together energeti-cally. "How much over and above a fair percentage did you get?"

"About five dollars."

"Good, again! You're a trump, Edward."

If Edward Claire was relieved to find that no suspicion had been awakened in the thoughts of Jasper, he did not feel very strongly flattered by his approving words. The truth was, at the very moment he was relating what he had done, there came into his mind, with a most startling distinctness, the dream of his wife, and the painful feelings it had occasioned.

"What folly! What madness! Whither am I going?"

These were his thoughts now, born of a quick revulsion of feeling.

"It is your dinner-time, Edward. Get back as soon as possible. I want to be home a little earlier than usual to-day."

Thus spoke Mr. Jasper; and the young man, taking up his hat, left the store. He had never felt so strangely in his life. The first step in crime had been taken; he had fairly entered the downward road to ruin. Where was it all to end? Placing his fingers, almost without thought, in his pocket, they came in contact with the gold-piece obtained by a double crime - the robbery both of a customer and his employer. Quickly, as if he had touched a living coal, was the hand of Claire withdrawn, while a low chill crept along his nerves. It required some resolution for the young man to meet his pure-hearted, clear-minded wife, whose quick intuitions of good or evil in others he had over and over again been led to remark. Once, as he moved along, he thrust his hand into his pocket, with the suddenly-formed purpose of casting the piece of money from him, and thus cancelling his guilt. But, ere the act was accomplished, he remembered that in this there would be no restoration, and so refrained.

Edward Claire felt, while in the presence of his young wife, that she often looked into his face with more than usual earnestness. This not only embarrassed but slightly fretted him, and led him to speak once in a way that brought tears to her eyes.

Not a minute longer than necessary did Claire remain at home. The fact that his employer had desired him to return to the store as quickly as possible, was an all-sufficient reason for his unusual hurry to get away.

The moment the door closed upon him, his wife burst into tears. On her bosom lay a most oppressive weight, and in her mind was a vague, troubled sense of approaching evil. She felt that there was dang er inthe path of her husband; but of its nature she could divine little or nothing. All day her dream had haunted her; and now it reproduced itself in her imagination with painful distinctness. Vainly she strove to drive it from her thoughts; it would not be gone. Slowly the hours wore on for her, until the deepening twilight brought the period when her husband was to return again. To this return her mind looked forward with an anxiety that could not be repressed.

The dreaded meeting with his wife over, Claire thought with less repugnance of what he had done, and was rather inclined to justify than condemn himself.

"It's the way of the world," so he argued; "and unless I do as the world does, I must remain where I am - at the bottom of the ladder. But why should I stay below, while all around me are struggling upward? As for what preachers and moralists call strictly fair dealing, it may be all well enough in theory, pleasant to talk about, and all that; but it won't do in practice, as the world now is. Where each is grasping all that he can lay his hands on, fair or foul, one must scramble with the rest, or get nothing. That is so plain that none can deny the proposition. So, Edward Claire, if you wish to rise above your present poor condition, if you wish to get rich, like your

T. S. Arthur

enterprising neighbours, you must do as they do. If I go in for a lamb, I might as well take a sheep: the morality of the thing is the same. If I take a large slice off of a customer, why shall not a portion of that slice be mine; ay, the whole of it, if I choose to make the appropriation? All Jasper can fairly ask, is a reasonable profit: if I, by my address, get more than this, surely I may keep a part thereof. Who shall say nay?"

Justifying himself by these and similar false reasonings, the young man thrust aside the better suggestions, from which he was at first inclined to retrace the false step he had taken; and wilfully shutting his eyes, resolved to go forward in his evil and dangerous course.

During the afternoon of that day a larger number of customers than usual were in, and Claire was very busily occupied. He made three or four large sales, and was successful in getting several dollars in excess of fair profit from one not very well skilled in prices. In making an entry of this particular transaction in the memorandum sales-book, the figures recorded were three dollars less than the actual amount received. So, on this, the first day of the young man's lapse from honesty, he had appropriated the sum of eight dollars - nearly equal to his entire week's salary! For such a recent traveller in this downward road, how rapid had already become his steps!

Evening found him again alone, musing and debating with himself, ere locking up the store and returning home. The excitement of business being over, his thoughts flowed in a calmer current; and the stillness of the deserted room gave to his feelings a hue of sobriety. He was not altogether satisfied with himself. How could he be? No man ever was satisfied with himself, when seclusion and silence found him after his first departure from the right way. Ah, how little is there in worldly possessions, be it large or small, to compensate for a troubled, self-accusing spirit! how little to throw in the balance against the heavy weight of conscious villany!

How tenderly, how truly, how devotedly had Edward Claire loved the young wife of his bosom, since the hour the pulses of their spirits first beat in joyful unity! How eager had he ever been to turn his face homeward when the shadows of evening began to fall! But now he lingered - lingered, though all the business of the day was over. The thought of his wife created no quick impulse to be away. He felt more like shunning her presence. He even for a time indulged a motion of anger toward her for what he mentally termed her morbid sensitiveness in regard to others' right - her dreamy ideal of human perfection.

"We are in the world, and we must do as it does. We must take it as it is, not as it should be."

So he mused with himself, in a self-approving argument. Yet he could not banish the accusing spirit; he could not silence the inward voice of warning.

Once there came a strong revulsion. Good impulses seemed about to gain the mastery. In this state of mind, he took from his pocket his ill-gotten gains, and threw them into the money-box, which had already been placed in the fire-closet.

"What good will that do?" said he to himself, as the wave of better feelings began to subside. "All the sales-entries have been made, and the cash balanced; Jasper made the balance himself. So the cash will only show an excess to be accounted for; and from this may come suspicion. It is always more hazardous to go backward than forward - (false reasoner!) - to retrace our steps than to press boldly onward. No, no. This will not mend the matter."

And Claire replaced the money in his pocket. In a little while afterward, he left the store, and took his way homeward.

T. S. Arthur

CHAPTER IV

As on the previous evening, Mrs. Claire was alone for some time later than usual, but now with an anxious, almost fearful looking for her husband's return. Suddenly she had taken the alarm. A deep, brooding shadow was on her heart, though she could not see the bird of night from whose wings it had fallen. Frequently, during the afternoon, tears had wet her cheek; and when an old friend of her mother's, who lived in the country, and who had come to the city in order to make a few purchases, called to see her, it was with difficulty she could hide her disturbed feelings from observation.

The absent one came in at last, and with so much of the old, frank, loving spirit in his voice and manner, that the troubled heart of Mrs. Claire beat with freer pulsations. And yet something about her husband appeared strange. There was a marked difference between his state of mind now, and on the evening before. Even at dinner-time he was silent and abstracted.

In fact, Edward Claire was, for the first time, acting a part toward his wife; and, as in all such cases, there was sufficient over-action to betray the artifice, or, at least, to awaken a doubt. Still, Edith was greatly relieved by the change, and she chided herself for having permitted doubt and vague questionings to find a harbour in her thoughts.

During tea-time, Claire chatted freely, as was his custom; but he grew serious as they sat together, after the table was cleared away, and Edith had taken her sewing. Then, for the first time, he thought out of himself sufficiently to remember his visit to the house of death in the morning, and he said -

"I witnessed something this morning, dear, that has made me feel sad ever since."

"What was that, Edward?" inquired the wife, looking instantly into his face, with a strongly manifested interest.

"I don't think you knew Mr. Elder or his family - Ruben Elder?"

"I have heard the name, nothing more."

"Mr. Elder died last week."

"Ah! What family did he leave?"

"A wife and one child."

Mrs. Claire sighed.

"Did he leave them comfortably off in the world?" she asked, after a brief silence.

"I don't know; but I'm afraid, he's not left much, if any thing. Mr. Jasper has been appointed the executor."

"Mr. Jasper!"

"Yes. This morning he called to see Mrs. Elder, and found her in a very low state. In fact, she died while he was there."

"Edward! Died?"

"Yes, died; and her only child, a sweet little girl, not five years old, is now a friendless orphan."

T. S. Arthur

"How very sad!"

"Sad enough, Edith, sad enough. Mr. Jasper, who has no taste for scenes of distress, wished me to look after the funeral arrangements; so I went to the house, and attended to matters as well as I could. Ah me! It has cast a gloom over my feelings that I find it hard to cast off."

"Did you see the child?" inquired Mrs. Claire, the mother's impulse giving direction to her thoughts.

"Yes; and a lovely child it is. Poor thing!"

"There are near relatives, I presume?"

"None; at least, so Jasper says."

"What is to become of the child?"

"Dear above knows! As for her legal guardian, she has nothing to hope from his humanity. She will naturally find a home somewhere - a home procured for money. But her future comfort and well-being will depend more on a series of happy accidents than on the good-will of the hard-hearted man to whose tender mercies the dying parents have committed her."

"Not happy accidents, Edward," said Mrs. Claire, with a tender smile; "say, wise providences. There is no such thing as chance."

"As you will, dear," returned the husband, with a slight change in his tone. "I would not call that providence wise by which Leonard Jasper became the guardian of a friendless child."

"This is because you cannot see the end from the beginning, Edward. The Lord's providence does not regard merely the external comfort and well-being of his creatures; it looks far beyond this, and regards their internal interests. It permits evil and suffering to-day, but only that good, a higher than earthly good, may come on the morrow. It was no blind chance, believe me, my husband, that led to the appointment of Mr. Jasper as the guardian of this poor child. Eternal purposes are involved therein, as surely as God is infinitely wise and good. Good to one, perhaps to many, will grow out of what now seems a deeply to be regretted circumstance."

"You're a happy reasoner, Edith. I wish I could believe in so consoling a philosophy."

"Edward!" There was a change in Mrs. Claire's voice, and a look blending surprise with a gentle rebuke in her countenance. "Edward, how can you speak so? Is not mine the plain Christian doctrine? Is it not to be found everywhere in the Bible?"

"Doubtless, Edith; but I'm not one of the pious kind, you know."

Claire forced a smile to his face, but his wife looked serious, and remarked -

"I don't like to hear you talk so, Edward. There is in it, to me, something profane. Ah, my dear husband, in this simple yet all-embracing doctrine of providence lies the whole secret of human happiness. If our Creator be infinite, wise, and good, he will seek the well-being of his creatures, even though they turn from him to do violence to his laws; and, in his infinite love and wisdom, will so order and arrange events as to make every thing conspire to the end in view. Both bodily and mental suffering are often permitted to take place, as the only agencies by which to counteract hereditary evils that would otherwise destroy the soul."

"Ah, Edie! Edie!" said Claire, interrupting his wife, in a fond, playful tone, "you are a wise preacher, and as good as you are wise. I only wish that I could see and feel as you do; no doubt it would be better for me in the end. But such a wish is vain."

"Oh, say not so, dear husband!" exclaimed Edith, with unexpected earnestness; "say not so! It hurts me almost like words of personal unkindness."

"But how can I be as good as you are? It isn't in me."

"I am not good, Edward. There is none good but God," answered the wife solemnly.

"Oh yes, yes! You are an angel!" returned Claire, with a sudden emotion that he could not control. "And I - and I - "

He checked himself, turned his face partly away to conceal its expression, sat motionless for a moment, and then burying his face on the bosom of his wife, sobbed for the space of nearly a minute, overcome by a passion that he in vain struggled to master.

Never had Edith seen her husband so moved. No wonder that she was startled, even frightened.

"Oh, Edward, dear Edward! what ails you?" were her eager, agitated words, so soon as she could speak. "What has happened? Oh, tell me, my husband, my dear husband!"

But Claire answered not, though he was gaining some control over his feelings.

"Oh, Edward! won't you speak to me? Won't you tell me all your troubles, all your heart? Am I not your wife, and do I not love you with a love no words can express? Am I not your best and closest friend? Would I not even lay down my life for your good? Dear Edward, what has caused this great emotion?"

Thus urged, thus pleaded the tearful Edith. But there was no reply, though the strong tremor which had thrilled through the frame of Claire had subsided. He was still bowed forward, with his face hid on her bosom, while her arm was drawn lovingly around him. So they remained for a time longer. At length, the young man lifted himself up, and fixed his eyes upon her. His countenance was pale and sad, and bore traces of intense suffering.

"My husband! my dear husband!" murmured Edith.

"My wife! my good angel!" was the low, thrilling response; and Claire pressed his lips almost reverently upon the brow of his wife.

"I have had a fearful dream, Edith!" said he; "a very fearful dream. Thank God, I am awake now."

"A dream, Edward?" returned his wife, not fully comprehending him.

"Yes, love, a dream; yet far too real. Surely, I dreamed, or was under some dire enchantment. But the spell is gone - gone, I trust, for ever."

"What spell, love? Oh, speak to me a plainer language!"

"I think, Edith," said the young man, after remaining thoughtfully silent for some time, "that I will try and get another place. I don't believe it is good for me to live with Leonard Jasper. Gold is the god he worships; and I find myself daily tempted to bend my knee in the same idolatry."

"Edward!" A shadow had fallen on the face of Edith.

"You look troubled at my words, Edith," resumed the young man; "yet what I say is true, too true. I wish it were not so. Ah! this passage through the world, hard and toilsome as it is, has many, many dangers."

"If we put our trust in God, we need have no fear," said Edith, in a gentle yet earnest and penetrating voice, laying her hand lovingly on the hot forehead of her husband, and gazing into his eyes.

T. S. Arthur

"Nothing without can harm us. Our worst enemies are within."

"Within?"

"Yes, love; within our bosoms. Into our distrusts and unsatisfied desires they enter, and tempt us to evil."

"True, true," said Claire, in an abstracted manner, and as if speaking to himself.

"What more do we want to make us happy?" asked Edith, comprehending still more clearly her husband's state of mind.

Claire sighed deeply, but made no answer.

"More money could not do it," she added.

"Money would procure us many comforts that we do not now possess," said the young man.

"I doubt this, Edward. It might give more of the elegancies of life; but, as I have often said, these do not always produce corresponding pleasure. If they come, without too ardent seeking, in the good pleasure of Providence, as the reward of useful and honest labour, then they may increase the delights of life; but never otherwise. If the heart is set on them, their acquirement will surely end in disappointment. Possession will create satiety; and the mind too quickly turns from the good it has toiled for in hope so long, to fret itself because there is an imagined higher good beyond. Believe me, Edward, if we are not satisfied with what God gives us as the reward of useful toil to-day, we will not be satisfied with what he gives to-morrow."

"Perhaps you are right, Edith; I believe you are. My mind has a glimpse of the truth, but to fully realize it is hard. Ah, I wish that I possessed more of your trusting spirit!"

"We are both cared for, Edward, by the same infinite love -

cared for, whether we doubt and fear, or trust confidingly."

"It must be so. I see it now, I feel it now - see it and feel it in the light of your clearer intuitions. Ah, how different from this pure faith is the faith of the world! Men worship gold as their god; they trust only in riches."

"And their god is ever mocking them. To-day he smiles upon his votary, and to-morrow hides his face in darkness. To-day he gives full coffers, that are empty to-morrow. But the true riches offered so freely to all by the living God are blessed both in the getting and in the keeping. These never produce satiety, never take to themselves wings. Good affections and true thoughts continually nourish and re-create the mind. They are the soul's wealth, the perennial fountains of all true enjoyment. With these, and sufficient for the body's health and comfort, all may be happy: without them, the riches of the world have no power to satisfy."

A pause ensued, during which the minds of both wandered back a little.

"If you feel," said Edith, recalling the words of her husband, "that there is danger in remaining where you are" -

"That was hastily spoken," Edward Claire interrupted his wife, "and in a moment of weakness. I must resist the evil that assaults me. I must strive with and overcome the tempter. I must think less of this world and its riches; and in my thoughts place a higher value upon the riches without wings of which you have spoken to me so often."

"Can you remain where you are, and be out of danger?" asked Edith.

"There is danger everywhere."

"Ay; but in some positions more imminent danger. Is it well to court temptation?"

T. S. Arthur

"Perhaps not. But I cannot afford to give up my place with Jasper."

"Yet, while remaining, you will be strongly tempted."

"Jasper is dishonest at heart. He is ever trying to overreach in dealing, and expects every one in his employment to be as keen as himself."

"Oh, Edward, do not remain with him a day longer! There is death to the spirit in the very atmosphere around such a man. You cannot serve such a master, and be true to yourself and to God. It is impossible."

"I believe you are right in that, Edith; I know you are right," said the young man, with a strong emphasis on the last sentence. "But what am I to do? Five hundred dollars a year is little enough for our wants; I have, as you know, been dissatisfied with that. I can hardly get as much in another situation. I know of but one opening, and that is with Melleville."

"Go back to him, Edward," said his wife.

"And get but four hundred a year? It is all he can pay."

"If but three hundred, it were a situation far to be preferred to the one you now hold."

"A hundred dollars a year, Edith, taken from our present income, would deprive us of many comforts."

"Think of how much we would gain in true inward enjoyment, Edward, by such a change. Have you grown happier since you entered the store of Mr. Jasper?"

The young man shook his head sadly, and murmured, "Alas! no."

"Can anything compensate for the anguish of mind we have both suffered in the last few hours, Edward?"

There was a quick flushing of the face, as Edith said this.

"Both suffered!" exclaimed Edward, with a look of surprise.

"Ay, both, love. Can the heart of my husband feel a jar of discord, and mine not thrill painfully? Can he be in temptation, without an overshadowing of my spirit? Can he be in darkness, and I at the same time in light? No, no; that were impossible. You have been in great peril; I knew that some evil threatened you, even before you confessed it with your lips. Oh, Edward, we have both tasted, in the last few hours, a bitterer cup than has yet been placed to our lips. May we not be called upon to drink it to the very dregs!"

"Amen!" fell solemnly from the lips of Edward Claire, as a cold shudder crept along his nerves. If there had been any wavering in his mind before, there was none now. He resolved to make restitution in the morning, and, as soon as opportunity offered, to leave a place where he was so strongly tempted to step aside from the path of integrity. The virtue of his wife had saved him.

CHAPTER V

"Edward," said Mr. Jasper, on the next morning, soon after he came to the store, "Was any time fixed for the funeral yesterday?"

"I believe not."

"That was an oversight. It might as well take place to-day as to-morrow, or a week hence, if there are no intimate friends or relatives to be thought of or consulted. I wish you would take the forenoon to see about this troublesome matter. The undertaker will, of course, do every thing according to your directions. Let there be as little expense as possible."

While they were yet speaking, the undertaker came in to make inquiry as to the funeral arrangements to be observed.

"Is the coffin ready?" asked Jasper, in a cold, business manner.

"It is," was the reply.

"What of the ground? Did you see to her husband's funeral?"

"Yes. I have attended to all these matters. Nothing remains but to fix the time, and notify the clergyman."

"Were you at the house this morning?" asked Jasper.

"I was."

"Who did you find there?"

"One or two of the neighbours were in."

"No near relatives of the deceased?"

"Not to my knowledge."

"Was any thing said about the time for burying Mrs. Elder?"

"No. That matter, I suppose, will rest with you."

"In that case, I see no reason for delay," said Jasper. "What end is served?"

"The sooner it is over the better."

"So I think. Suppose we say this afternoon?"

"Very well. The time might be fixed at five. The graveyard is not very distant. How many carriages shall I order?"

"Not many. Two, I should think, would be enough," replied Jasper. "There will not be much left, I presume; therefore, the lighter the funeral expenses the better. By the way, did you see the child, when you were there this morning?"

"No, sir."

"Some neighbour has, in all probability, taken it."

"Very likely. It is a beautiful child."

"Yes - rather pretty," was Jasper's cold response.

"So young to be left alone in the world. Ah, me! But these things will happen. So, you decide to have the funeral at five this afternoon?"

T. S. Arthur

"Yes; unless something that we do not now know of, interferes to prevent. The quicker a matter like this is over the better."

"True. Very well."

"You will see to every thing?"

"Certainly; that is my business. Will you be at the house this afternoon?"

"At the time of the funeral?"

"Yes."

"I think not. I can't do any good."

"No, - only for the looks of the thing."

The undertaker was already beginning to feel the heartless indifference of Jasper, and his last remark was half in irony, half in smothered contempt.

"Looks! Oh! I never do any thing for looks. If I can be of any service, I will be there - but, if not, not. I'm a right up-and-down, straight-forward man of the world, you see."

The undertaker bowed, saying that all should be as he wished.

"You can step around there, after a while, Edward," said Jasper, as soon as the undertaker had retired. "When you go, I wish you would ascertain, particularly, what has been done with the child. If a neighbour has taken her home, make inquiry as to whether she will be retained in the family; or, better still, adopted. You can hint, in a casual way, you know, that her parents have left property, which may, some time or other, be valuable. This may be a temptation, and turn the scale in favour of adoption; which may save me a world of trouble and responsibility."

"There is some property left?" remarked Claire.

"A small house or two, and a bit of worthless land in the mountains. All, no doubt, mortgaged within a trifle of their value. Still, it's property you know; and the word 'property' has a very attractive sound in some people's ears."

A strong feeling of disgust toward Jasper swelled in the young man's heart, but he guarded against its expression in look or words.

A customer entering at the moment, Claire left his principal and moved down behind the counter. He was not very agreeably affected, as the lady approached him, to see in her the person from whom he had taken ten dollars on the previous day, in excess of a reasonable profit. Her serious face warned him that she had discovered the cheat.

"Are you the owner of this store?" she asked, as she leaned upon the counter, and fixed her mild, yet steady eyes, upon the young man's face.

"I am not, ma'am," replied Claire, forcing a smile as he spoke. "Didn't I sell you a lot of goods yesterday?"

"You did, sir."

"I thought I recognised you. Well, ma'am, there was an error in your bill - an overcharge."

"So I should think."

"A overcharge of five dollars."

Claire, while he affected an indifferent manner, leaned over toward the woman and spoke in a low tone of voice. Inwardly, he was trembling lest Jasper should became cognizant of what was passing.

T. S. Arthur

"Will you take goods for what is due you; or shall I hand you back the money?" said he.

"As I have a few more purchases to make, I may as well take goods," was replied, greatly to the young man's relief.

"What shall I show you, ma'am?" he asked, in a voice that now reached the attentive ears of Jasper, who had been wondering to himself as to what was passing between the clerk and customer.

A few articles were mentioned, and, in a little while, another bill of seven dollars was made.

"I am to pay you two dollars, I believe?" said the lady, after Claire had told her how much the articles came to. As she said this, Jasper was close by and heard the remark.

"Right, ma'am," answered the clerk.

The customer laid a ten-dollar bill on the counter. Claire saw that the eyes of Jasper were on him. He took it up, placed it in the money-drawer, and stood some time fingering over the change and small bills. Then, with his back turned toward Jasper, he slipped a five dollar gold piece from his pocket. This, with a three dollar bill from the drawer, he gave to the lady, who received her change and departed.

Other customers coming in at the moment, both Jasper and his clerk were kept busy for the next hour. When they were alone again, the former said -

"How large a bill did you sell the old lady from the country, who was in this morning?"

"The amount was seven dollars, I believe."

"I thought she said two dollars?"

"She gave me a ten-dollar bill, and I only took three from the drawer," said the young man.

"I thought you gave her a piece of gold?"

"There was no gold in the drawer," was replied, evasively,

Much to the relief of Claire, another customer entered, thus putting an end to the conference between him and Jasper.

The mind of the latter, ever suspicious, was not altogether satisfied. He was almost sure that two dollars was the price named for the goods, and that he had seen a gold coin offered in change. And he took occasion to refer to it at the next opportunity, when his clerk's positive manner, backed by the entry of seven dollars on the sales' book, silenced him.

As for Claire, this act of restitution, so far as it was in his power to make it, took from his mind a heavy burden. He had, still, three dollars in his possession that were not rightfully his own. It was by no means probable that a similar opportunity to the one just embraced would occur. What then was it best for him to do? This question was soon after decided, by his throwing the money into the cash-drawer of Jasper.

On his way home to dinner that day, Claire called into the store of a Mr. Melleville, referred to in the conversation with his wife on the previous evening. This gentleman, who was somewhat advanced in years, was in the same business with Jasper. He was known as a strictly upright dealer - "Too honest to get along in this world," as some said. "Old Stick-in-the-mud," others called him. "A man behind the times," as the new-comers in the trade were pleased to say. Claire had lived with him for some years, and left him on the offer of Jasper to give him a hundred dollars more per annum than he was getting.

"Ah, Edward! How do you do to-day?" said Mr. Melleville, kindly, as the young man came in.

"Very well in body, but not so well in mind," was the frank reply, as he took the proffered hand of his old employer.

"Not well in mind, ah! That's about the worst kind of sickness I know of, Edward. What's the matter?"

"As I have dropped in to talk with you a little about my own affairs, I will come at once to the point."

"That is right. Speak out plainly, Edward, and you will find in me, at least, a sincere friend, and an honest adviser. What is the matter now?"

"I don't like my present situation, Mr. Melleville!"

"Ah! Well? What's the trouble? Have you and Jasper had a misunderstanding?"

"Oh no! Nothing of that. We get on well enough together. But I don't think its a good place for a young man to be in, sir!"

"Why not?"

"I can be plain with you. In a word, Mr. Jasper is not an honest dealer; and he expects his clerks to do pretty much as he does."

Mr. Melleville shook his head and looked grave.

"To tell the truth," continued Edward, "I have suffered myself to fall, almost insensibly, into his way of doing business, until I have become an absolute cheat - taking, sometimes, double and treble profit from a customer who happened to be ignorant about prices."

"Edward!" exclaimed the old man, an expression of painful surprise settling on his countenance.

"It is all too true, Mr. Melleville - all too true. And I don't think it good for me to remain with Mr. Jasper."

"What does he give you now?"

"The same as at first. Five hundred dollars."

The old man bent his head and thought for a few moments.

"His system of unfair dealing toward his customers is your principal objection to Mr. Jasper?"

"That is one objection, and a very serious one, too: particularly as I am required to be as unjust to customers as himself. But there is still another reason why I wish to get away from this situation. Mr. Jasper seems to think and care for nothing but money-getting. In his mind, gold is the highest good. To a far greater extent than I was, until very recently, aware, have I fallen, by slow degrees, into his way of thinking and feeling; until I have grown dissatisfied with my position. Temptation has come, as a natural result; and, before I dreamed that my feet were wandering from the path of safety, I have found myself on the brink of a fearful precipice."

"My dear young friend!" said Mr. Melleville, visibly moved, "this is dreadful!"

"It is dreadful. I can scarcely realize that it is so," replied Claire, also exhibiting emotion.

"You ought not to remain in the employment of Leonard Jasper. That, at least, is plain. Better, far better, to subsist on bread and water, than to live sumptuously on the ill-gotten gold of such a man."

"Yes, yes, Mr. Melleville, I feel all the truth of what you affirm, and am resolved to seek for another place. Did you not say, when we parted two years ago, that if ever I wished to return, you would endeavour to make an opening for me?"

"I did, Edward; and can readily bring you in now, as one of my young men is going to leave me for a higher salary than I can afford to pay. There is one drawback, however."

"What is that, Mr. Melleville?"

"The salary will be only four hundred dollars a year."

"I shall expect no more from you."

"But can you live on that sum now? Remember, that you have been receiving five hundred dollars, and that your wants have been graduated by your rate of income. Let me ask - have you saved any thing since you were married?"

"Nothing."

"So much the worse. You will find it difficult to fall back upon a reduced salary. How far can you rely on your wife's co-operation?"

"To the fullest extent. I have already suggested to her the change, and she desires, above all things, that I make it."

"Does she understand the ground of this proposed change?" asked Mr. Melleville.

"Clearly."

"And is willing to meet privation - to step down into even a humbler sphere, so that her husband be removed from the tempting influence of the god of this world?"

"She is, Mr. Melleville. Ah! I only wish that I could look upon life as she does. That I could see as clearly - that I could gather, as she is gathering them in her daily walk, the riches that have no wings."

"Thank God for such a treasure, Edward! She is worth more

than the wealth of the Indies. With such an angel to walk by your side, you need feel no evil."

"You will give me a situation, then, Mr. Melleville?"

"Yes, Edward," replied the old man.

"Then I will notify Mr. Jasper this afternoon, and enter your service on the first of the coming month. My heart is lighter already. Good day."

And Edward hurried off home.

During the afternoon he found no opportunity to speak to Mr. Jasper on the subject first in his thoughts, as that individual wished him to attend Mrs. Elder's funeral, and gather for him all possible information about the child. It was late when he came back from the burial-ground - so late that he concluded not to return, on that evening, to the store. In the carriage in which he rode, was the clergyman who officiated, and the orphan child who, though but half comprehending her loss, was yet overwhelmed with sorrow. On their way back, the clergyman asked to be left at his own dwelling; and this was done. Claire was then alone with the child, who shrank close to him in the carriage. He did not speak to her; nor did she do more than lift, now and then, her large, soft, tear-suffused eyes to his face.

Arrived, at length, at the dwelling from which they had just borne forth the dead, Claire gently lifted out the child, and entered the house with her. Two persons only were within, the domestic and the woman who, on the day previous, had spoken of taking to her own home the little orphaned one. The former had on her shawl and bonnet, and said that she was about going away.

"You will not leave this child here alone," said Edward.

"I will take her for the present," spoke up the other. "Would you like to go home with me, Fanny?" addressing the child. "Come," - and she held out her hands.

But the child shrank closer to the side of Edward, and looked up into his face with a silent appeal that his heart could not resist.

"Thank you, ma'am," he returned politely. "But we won't trouble you to do that. I will take her to my own home for the present. Would you like to go with me, dear?"

Fanny answered with a grateful look, as she lifted her beautiful eyes again to his face.

And so, after the woman and the domestic had departed, Edward Claire locked up the house, and taking the willing child by the hand, led her away to his own humble dwelling.

Having turned himself resolutely away from evil, already were the better impulses of his nature quickened into active life. A beautiful humanity was rising up to fill the place so recently about to be consecrated to the worship of a hideous selfishness.

CHAPTER VI

Edward Claire was in no doubt as to the reception the motherless child would receive from his kind-hearted wife. A word or two of explanation enabled her to comprehend the feeling from which he had acted.

"You were right, Edward," said she in hearty approval. "I am glad you brought her home. Come, dear," speaking to the wondering, partly shrinking orphan, "let me take off your bonnet."

She kissed the child's sweet lips and then gazed for some moments into her face, pleased, yet half surprised, at her remarkable beauty.

Little Fanny felt that she was among friends. The sad expression of her face soon wore off, light came back to her eyes, and her prattling tongue released itself from a long silence. An hour afterward, when she was laid to sleep in a temporary bed, made for her on the floor, her heavy eyelids fell quickly, with their long lashes upon her cheeks, and she was soon in the world of dreams.

Then followed a long and serious conference between Edward and his wife.

"I saw Mr. Melleville to-day," said the former.

"Did you? I am glad of that," was answered.

T. S. Arthur

"He will give me a place."

"Glad again."

"But, Edith, as I supposed, he can only pay me a salary of four hundred dollars."

"No matter," was the prompt reply; "it is better than five hundred where you are."

"Can we live on it, Edith?" Edward spoke in a troubled voice.

"Why not? It is but to use a little more economy in our expenses - to live on two dollars a week less than we now spend; and that will not be very hard to do. Trust it to me, dear. I will bring the account out even. And we will be just as happy. As happy? Oh, a thousand times happier! A hundred dollars! How poorly will that compensate for broken peace and a disquieted conscience. Edward, is it possible for you to remain where you are, and be innocent?"

"I fear not, Edith," was the unhesitating reply. "And yet, dear, I should be man enough, should have integrity enough, to resist the temptations that might come in my way."

"Do not think of remaining where you are," said the young wife earnestly. "If Mr. Melleville will pay you four hundred dollars a year, take his offer and leave Mr. Jasper. It will be a gain rather than a loss to us."

"A gain, Edith?"

"Yes, a gain in all that is worth having in life - peace of mind flowing from a consciousness of right action. Will money buy this? No, Edward. Highly as riches are esteemed - the one great good in life as they are regarded - they never have given and never will give this best of all blessings. How little, how very little of the world's happiness, after all, flows from the possession of money. Did you ever think of that, Edward?"

"Perhaps not."

"And yet, is it not worth a passing thought? Mr. and Mrs. Casswell are rich - we are poor. Which do you think the happiest?"

"Oh, we are happiest, a thousand times," said Edward warmly. "I would not exchange places with him, were he worth a million for every thousand."

"Nor I with his wife," returned Edith. "So money, in their case, does not give happiness. Now look at William Everhart and his wife. When we were married they occupied two rooms, at a low rent, as we now do. Their income was just what ours has been. Well, they enjoyed life. We visited them frequently, and they often called to see us. But for a little ambition on the part of both to make some show, they would have possessed a large share of that inestimable blessing, contentment. After a while, William's salary was raised to one thousand dollars. Then they must have a whole house to themselves, as if their two nice rooms were not as large and comfortable, and as well suited to their real wants as before. They must, also, have showy furniture for their friends to look at. Were they any happier for this change? - for this marked improvement in their external condition? We have talked this over before, Edward. No, they were not. In fact, they were not so comfortable. With added means had come a whole train of clamorous wants, that even the doubled salary could not supply."

"Everhart gets fifteen hundred a year, now," remarked Claire.

"That will account, then," said Edith, smiling, "for Emma's unsettled state of mind when I last saw her. New wants have been created; and they have disturbed the former tranquillity."

"All are not so foolish as they have been. I think we might bear an increased income without the drawbacks that have attended theirs."

T. S. Arthur

"If it had been best for us, my husband, God would have provided it. It is in his loving-kindness that he has opened the way so opportunely for you to leave the path of doubt and danger for one of confidence and safety; and, in doing it, he has really increased your salary."

"Increased it, Edith! Why do you say that?"

"Will we not be happier for the change?" asked Edith, smiling.

"I believe so."

"Then, surely, the salary is increased by so much of heartfelt pleasure. Why do you desire an increase rather than a diminution of income?"

"In order to procure more of the comforts of life," was answered.

"Comfort for the body, and satisfaction for the mind?"

"Yes."

"Could our bodies really enjoy more than they now enjoy? They are warmly clothed, fully fed, and are in good health. Is it not so?"

"It is."

"Then, if by taking Mr. Melleville's offer, you lose nothing for the body, and gain largely for the mind, is not your income increased?"

"Ah, Edith!" said Claire, fondly, "you are a wonderful reasoner. Who will gainsay such arguments?"

"Do I not argue fairly? Are not my positions sound, and my deductions clearly brought forth?"

"If I could always see and feel as I do now," said Claire, in a low, pleased tone of voice, "how smoothly would life glide onward. Money is not every thing. Ah! how fully that is seen. There are possessions not to be bought with gold."

"And they are mental possessions - states of the mind, Edward," spoke up Edith quickly. "Riches that never fade, nor fail; that take to themselves no wings. Oh, let us gather of these abundantly, as we walk on our way through life."

"Heaven has indeed blessed me." Such was the heartfelt admission of Edward Claire, made in the silence of his own thoughts. "With a different wife - a lover of the world and its poor vanities - how imminent would have been my danger! Alas! scarcely any thing less than a miracle would have saved me. I shudder as I realize the fearful danger through which I have just passed. I thank God for so good a wife."

The first inquiry made by Jasper, when he met Edward on the next morning, was in relation to what he had seen at the funeral, and, particularly, as to the disposition that had been made of the child.

"I took her home with me," was replied, in answer to a direct question.

"You did!" Jasper seemed taken by surprise. "How came that, Edward?"

"When I returned from the cemetery, I found the domestic ready to leave the house. Of course the poor child could not remain there alone; so I took her home with me for the night."

"How did your wife like that?" asked Jasper, with something in his tone that showed a personal interest in the reply.

"Very well. I did just what she would have done under the circumstances."

"You have only one child, I believe?" said Jasper, after a pause of some moments.

"That is all."

"Only three in family?"

"Only three."

"How would you like to increase it? Suppose you keep this child of Elder's, now she is with you. I have been looking a little into the affairs of the estate, and find that there are two houses, unincumbered, that are rented each for two hundred and fifty dollars a year. Of course, you will receive a reasonable sum for taking care of the child. What do you say to it? As executor, I will pay you five dollars a week for boarding and clothing her until she is twelve years of age. After that, a new arrangement can be made."

"I can't give an answer until I consult my wife," said Claire, in reply to so unexpected a proposition.

"Urge her to accept the offer, Edward. Just think what it will add to your income. I'm sure it won't cost you one-half the sum, weekly, that I have specified, to find the child in every thing."

"Perhaps not. But all will depend on my wife. We are living, now, in two rooms, and keep no domestic. An addition of one to our family might so increase her care and labour as to make a servant necessary. Then we should have to have an additional room; the rent of which and the wages and board of the servant would amount to nearly as much as we would receive from you on account of the child."

"Yes, I see that," returned Jasper. And he mused for some moments. He was particularly anxious that Claire should take the orphan, for then all the trouble of looking after and caring for her would be taken from him, and that would be a good deal gained.

"I'll tell you what, Edward," he added. "If you will take her, I will call the sum six dollars a week - or three hundred a year. That will make the matter perfectly easy. If your wife does not seem at first inclined, talk to her seriously. This addition to your income will be a great help. To show her that I am perfectly in earnest, and that you can depend on receiving the sum specified, I will draw up a little agreement, which, if all parties are satisfied, can be signed at once."

Claire promised to talk the matter over with his wife at dinner-time.

The morning did not pass without varied assaults upon the young man's recent good resolutions. Several times he had customers in from whom it would have been easy to get more than a fair profit, but he steadily adhered to what he believed to be right, notwithstanding Jasper once or twice expressed dissatisfaction at his not having made better sales, and particularly at his failing to sell a piece of cloth, because he would not pledge his word as to its colour and quality - neither of which were good.

The proposition of Jasper for him to make, in his family, a place for the orphan, caused Claire to postpone the announcement of his intention to leave his service, until after he had seen and conferred with his wife.

At the usual dinner-hour, Claire returned home. His mind had become by this time somewhat disturbed. The long-cherished love of money, subdued for a brief season, was becoming active again. Here were six dollars to be added, weekly, to his income, provided his wife approved the arrangement, - and it was to come through Jasper. The more he thought of this increase, the more his natural cupidity was stirred, and the less willing he felt to give up the proposed one hundred dollars in his salary. If he persisted in leaving Jasper, there would, in all probability, be a breach between them, and this would, he felt

T. S. Arthur

certain, prevent an arrangement that he liked better and better the more he thought about it. He was in this state of mind when he arrived at home.

On pushing open the door of their sitting-room, the attention of Claire was arrested by the animated expression of his wife's face. She raised her finger to enjoin silence. Tripping lightly to his side, she drew her arm within his, and whispered -

"Come into the chamber, dear - tread softly - there, isn't that sweet? - isn't it lovely?"

The sight was lovely indeed. A pillow had been thrown on the floor, and upon this lay sleeping, arm in arm, the two children. Pressed close together were their rosy cheeks; and the sunny curls of Fanny Elder were mixed, like gleams of sunshine, amid the darker ringlets that covered profusely the head of little Edith.

"Did you ever see any thing so beautiful?" said the delighted mother.

"What a picture it would make!" remarked Edward, who was charmed with the sight.

"Oh, lovely! How I would like just such a picture!"

"She is a beautiful child," said Edward.

"Very," was the hearty response. "Very - and so sweet-tempered and winning in her ways. Do you know, I am already attached to her. And little Edie is so delighted. They have played all the morning like kittens; and a little while ago lay down, just as you see them - tired out, I suppose - and fell off to sleep. It must have been hard for the mother to part with that child - hard, very hard."

And Mrs. Claire sighed.

"You will scarcely be willing to give her up, if she remains here long," said Edward.

"I don't know how I should feel to part from her, even now. Oh, isn't it sad to think that she has no living soul to love or care for her in the world."

"Mr. Jasper is her guardian, you know."

"Yes; and such a guardian!"

"I should not like to have my child dependent on his tender mercies, certainly. But he will have little to do with her beyond paying the bills for her maintenance. He will place her in some family to board; and her present comfort and future well-being will depend very much upon the character of the persons who have charge of her."

Edith sighed.

"I wish," said she, after a pause, "that we were able to take her. But we are not."

And she sighed again.

"Mr. Jasper will pay six dollars a week to any one who will take the entire care of her until she is twelve years of age."

"Will he?" A sudden light had gleamed over the face of Mrs. Claire.

"Yes; he said so this morning."

"Then, why may not we take her? I am willing," was Edith's quick suggestion.

"It is a great care and responsibility," said Edward.

"I shall not feel it so. When the heart prompts, duty becomes a pleasure. O yes, dear, let us take the child by all means."

"Can we make room for her?"

"Why not? Her little bed, in a corner of our chamber, will in noway incommode us; and through the day she will be a companion for Edie. If you could only have seen how sweetly they played together! Edie has not been half the trouble to-day that she usually is."

"It will rest altogether with you, Edith," said Claire, seriously. "In fact, Mr. Jasper proposed that we should take Fanny. I did not give him much encouragement, however."

"Have you any objection, dear?" asked Edith.

"None. The sum to be paid weekly will more than cover the additional cost of housekeeping. If you are prepared for the extra duties that must come, I have nothing to urge against the arrangement."

"If extra duties are involved, I will perform them as a labour of love. Without the sum to be paid for the child's maintenance, I would have been ready to take her in and let her share our home. She is now in the special guardianship of the Father of the fatherless, and he will provide for her, no matter who become the almoners of his bounty. This is my faith, Edward, and in this faith I would have freely acted even without the provision that has been made."

"Let it be then, as you wish, Edith."

"How providential this increase of our income, Edward!" said his wife, soon afterward, while the subject of taking Fanny into their little household was yet the burden of their conversation. "We shall gain here all, and more than all that will be lost in giving up your situation with Mr. Jasper. Did I not say to you that good would come of this guardianship; and is there not, even now, a foreshadowing of things to come?"

"Perhaps there is," replied Edward thoughtfully. "But my eye of faith is not so clear as yours."

"Let me see for you then, dear," said Edith, in a tender voice. "I am an earnest confider in the good purposes of our Heavenly Father. I trust in them, as a ship trusts in its well-grounded anchor. That, in summing up the events of our life, when the time of our departure comes, we shall see clearly that each has been wisely ordered or provided for by One who is infinitely good and wise, I never for an instant doubt. Oh, if you could only see with me, eye to eye, Edward! But you will, love, you will - that my heart assures me. It may be some time yet - but it will come."

"May it come right speedily!" was the fervent response of Edward Claire.

T. S. Arthur

CHAPTER VII

"Well, Edward, what does your wife say?" Such was the inquiry of Jasper, immediately on the return of his clerk from dinner.

"There will be no difficulty, so far as she is concerned," the young man answered.

"None, did you say, Edward?"

"None. She is willing to take the child, under the arrangement you propose."

"That is, for three hundred dollars a year, to find her in every thing?"

"Yes; until she is twelve years of age."

"So I understand it. After that, as the expense of her clothing and education will increase, we can make a new arrangement. Very well. I'm glad you have decided to take the child. It won't cost you six dollars a week, for the present, I am sure: so the additional income will be quite a help to you."

"I don't know how that will be. At any rate, we are willing to take the child into our family."

"Suppose then, Edward, we mutually sign this little agreement to that effect, which I have drawn up."

And Jasper took a paper from his desk, which he handed to Edward.

"I've no objection," said the latter, after he had read it over. "It binds me to the maintenance of the child until she is twelve years of age, and you to the payment therefor of three hundred dollars a year, in quarterly payments of seventy-five dollars each."

"Yes, that is the simple statement of the matter. You see, I have prepared duplicates: one for you, and one for myself. I will sign them first."

And Jasper took a pen and placed upon each of the documents his sign-manual.

Claire did the same; and a clerk witnessed the signatures. Each, then, took a copy. Thus, quickly and fully, was the matter arranged.

This fact of giving to the contract a legal form, was, under the circumstances, the very thing Claire most desired. He had already begun to see difficulties ahead, so soon as he announced his intention of leaving Jasper's service; particularly, as no reason that he could give would satisfy the merchant - difficulties growing out of this new relation as the personal guardian of little Fanny Elder. The signing of a regular contract for the payment of a certain sum of money, quarterly, for the child's maintenance, gave him a legal right to collect that sum, should Jasper, from any change of feeling, be disposed at some future time to give him trouble. This was something gained.

It was with exceeding reluctance that Claire forced himself, during the afternoon, to announce his intention to leave Mr. Jasper. Had he not promised Mr. Melleville and his wife to do this, it would certainly have been postponed for the present; perhaps altogether. But his word was passed to both of them, and he felt that to defer the matter would be wrong. So, an

T. S. Arthur

opportunity offering, he said -

"I believe, Mr. Jasper, that I shall have to leave you."

"Leave me, Edward!" Mr. Jasper was taken altogether by surprise. "What is the meaning of this? You have expressed no dissatisfaction. What is wrong?"

The position of Edward was a trying one. He could not state the true reasons for wishing to leave his present situation, without giving great offence, and making, perhaps, an enemy. This he wished, if possible, to avoid. A few days before he would not have scrupled at the broadest equivocation, or even at a direct falsehood. But there had been a birth of better principles in his mind, and he was in the desire to let them govern his conduct. As he did not answer promptly the question of Jasper as to his reasons for wishing to leave him, the latter said -

"This seems to be some sudden purpose, Edward. Are you going to receive a higher salary?"

Still Edward did not reply; but looked worried and irresolute. Taking it for granted that no motive but a pecuniary one could have prompted this desire for change, Jasper continued -

"I have been satisfied with you, Edward. You seem to understand me, and to comprehend my mode of doing business. I have found you industrious, prompt, and cheerful in performing your duties. These are qualities not always to be obtained. I do not, therefore, wish to part with you. If a hundred, or even a hundred and fifty dollars a year, will be any consideration, your salary is increased from to-day."

This, to Edward, was unexpected. He felt more bewildered and irresolute than at first. So important an advance in his income, set against a reduction of the present amount, was a strong temptation, and he felt his old desires for money arraying themselves in his mind.

"I will think over your offer," said he. "I did not expect this. In the morning I will be prepared to decide."

"Very well, Edward. If you remain, your salary will be increased to six hundred and fifty dollars."

To Claire had now come another hour of darkness. The little strength, just born of higher principles, was to be sorely tried. Gold was in one scale, and the heavenly riches that are without wings in the other. Which was to overbalance?

The moment Claire entered the presence of his wife, on returning home that evening, she saw that a change had taken place - an unfavourable change; and a shadow fell upon her pure spirit.

"I spoke to Mr. Jasper about leaving him," he remarked, soon after he came in.

"What did he say?" inquired Edith.

"He does not wish me to go."

"I do not wonder at that. But, of course, he is governed merely by a selfish regard to his own interests."

"He offers to increase my salary to six hundred and fifty dollars," said Edward, in a voice that left his wife in no doubt as to the effect which this had produced.

"A thousand dollars a year, Edward," was the serious answer, "would be a poor compensation for such services as he requires. Loss of self-respect, loss of honour, loss of the immortal soul, are all involved. Think of this, my dear husband! and do not for a moment hesitate."

But Edward did hesitate. This unexpected offer of so important an increase in his salary had excited his love of money, temporarily quiescent. He saw in such an increase a

T. S. Arthur

great temporal good; and this obscured his perception of a higher good, which, a little while before, had been so clear.

"I am not so sure, Edith," said he, "that all these sad consequences are necessarily involved. I am under no obligation to deal unfairly with his customers. My duty will be done, when I sell to them all I can at a fair profit. If he choose to take an excess of profit in his own dealing, that is his affair. I need not be partaker in his guilt."

"Edward!" returned his wife, laying her hand upon his arm, and speaking in a low, impressive voice - "Do you really believe that you can give satisfaction to Mr. Jasper in all things, and yet keep your conscience void of offence before God and man? Think of his character and requirements - think of the kind of service you have, in too many instances, rendered him - and then say whether it will be possible to satisfy him without putting in jeopardy all that a man should hold dear - all that is worth living for? Oh, Edward! do not let this offer blind you for a moment to the real truth."

"Then you would have me reject the offer?"

"Without an instant's hesitation, Edward."

"It is a tempting one. And then, look at the other side, Edith. Only four hundred dollars a year, instead of six hundred and fifty."

"I feel it as no temptation. The latter sum, in the present case, is by far the better salary, for it will give us higher sources of enjoyment. What are millions of dollars, and a disquiet mind, compared to a few hundreds, and sweet peace? If you remain with Jasper, an unhappy spirit will surely steal into our dwelling - if you take, for the present, your old place with Mr. Melleville, how brightly will each morning's sun shine in upon us, and how calmly will the blessed evening draw around her curtains of repose!"

Edith had always possessed great influence over her husband. He loved her very tenderly; and was ever loth to do any thing to which she made opposition. She was no creature of mere impulse - of weak caprices - of captious, yet unbending will. If she opposed her husband in any thing, it was on the ground of its non-agreement with just principles; and she always sustained her positions with the clearest and most direct modes of argumentation. Not with elaborate reasonings, but rather in the declaration of things self-evident - the quick perceptions of a pure, truth-loving mind. How inestimable the blessing of such a wife!

"No doubt you have the better reason on your side, Edith," replied her husband, his manner very much subdued. "But it is difficult for me to unclasp my hand to let fall therefrom the natural good which I can see and estimate, for the seemingly unreal and unsubstantial good that, to your purer vision, looms up so imposingly."

"Unreal - unsubstantial - Edward!" said Edith, in reply to this. "Are states of mind unreal?"

"I have not always found them so," was answered.

"Is happiness, or misery, unreal? Oh, are they not our most palpable realizations? It is not mere wealth that is sought for as an end - that is not the natural good for which the many are striving. It is the mental enjoyment that possession promises - the state of mind that would be gained through gold as a means. Is it not so? Think."

"Yes - that is, undoubtedly, the case."

"But, is it possible for money to give peace and true enjoyment, if, in the spirit, even though not in the letter, violence is done to the laws of both God and man? Can ill-gotten gain produce heavenly beatitudes? - and there are none others. The heart never grows truly warm and joyous except when light from above streams through the darkened vapours

T. S. Arthur

with which earth-fires have surrounded it. Oh, my husband! Turn yourself away from this world's false allurements, and seek with me the true riches. Whatever may be your lot in life - I care not how poor and humble - I shall walk erect and cheerful by your side if you have been able to keep a conscience void of offence; but if this be not so, and you bring to me gold and treasure without stint, my head will lie bowed upon my bosom, and my heart throb in low, grief-burdened pulsations. False lights, believe me, Edward, are hung out by the world, and they lure life's mariner on to dangerous coasts. Let us remain on a smooth and sunny sea, while we can, and not tempt the troubled and uncertain wave, unless duty requires the venture. Then, with virtue at the helm, and the light of God's love in the sky, we will find a sure haven at last."

"It shall be as you wish, Edith," said Claire, as he gazed with admiring affection into the bright and glowing face of his wife, that was lovely in her beautiful enthusiasm.

"No - no, Edward! Don't say as *I* wish," was her quick reply. "I cannot bear that you should act merely under my influence as an external pressure. If I have seemed to use persuasion, it has not been to force you over to my way of thinking. But, cannot you see that I am right? Does not your reason approve of what I say?"

"It does, Edith. I can see, as well as feel, that you are right. But, the offer of a present good is a strong temptation. I speak freely."

"And I thank you for doing so. Oh! never conceal from me your inmost thoughts. You say that you can see as well as feel that I am right?"

"Yes; I freely acknowledge that."

"Your reason approves what I have said?"

"Fully."

"This tells you that it will be better for you in the end to accept of four hundred dollars from Mr. Melleville, than to remain with Mr. Jasper at six hundred and fifty?"

"It does, Edith."

"Then, my husband, let the reason which God has given to you as a guide, direct you now in the right way. Do not act under influence from me - for then the act will not be freely your own - but, as a truly rational, and, therefore, a wise man, choose now the way in which an enlightened reason tells you that you ought to walk."

"I have chosen, Edith," was the young man's low, but firm reply.

"How?" The wife spoke with a sudden, trembling eagerness, and held her breath for an answer.

"I will leave my present place, and return to Mr. Melleville."

"God be thanked!" came sobbing from the lips of Edith, as she threw herself in unrestrained joy upon the bosom of her husband.

CHAPTER VIII

"I don't just understand this," said Jasper to himself, after the interview with his clerk described in another chapter. "I thought him perfectly satisfied. He didn't say he was offered a higher salary. Ah! guess I've got it now. It's only a bit of a ruse on his part to get me to increase his wages. I didn't think of this before. Well, it has succeeded; and, in truth, he's worth all I've offered him. Shrewd, quick, and sharp; he's a young man just to my mind. Should he grow restless again, I must tempt him with the idea of a partnership at some future period. If business goes on increasing, I shall want some one with me whom I can trust and depend on more fully than on a clerk."

Thus, in the mind of Jasper, all was settled; and he was fully prepared, on the next morning, when he met Edward to hear from him that he would remain in his service. A different decision took him altogether by surprise.

"Where are you going?" he asked. Edward hesitated a moment ere replying.

"Back to Mr. Melleville's."

"To Melleville's! Will he give you more salary than I have agreed to pay?"

"No," was the answer; "but I have reasons for wishing to accept the place he offers me."

"Well, just as you please," said Jasper, coldly. "Every one must suit himself."

And, with the air of a person offended, he turned himself from the young man. Soon after he went out, and did not come back for two or three hours. When he re-entered the store there was an angry flash in his eyes, which rested somewhat sternly upon Claire.

"Let me say a word with you, Edward."

There happened to be no customer in to engage the clerk's attention, and he retired, with his employer, to the back part of the store. Jasper then turned and confronted him with a stern aspect.

"Well, young man!" said he sharply, "it seems that you have been making rather free with my good name, of late; representing me as a cheat and a swindler."

For a few moments the mind of Claire was strongly excited and in a perfect maze of confusion. The blood mounted to his face, and he felt a rising and choking sensation in his throat. Wisely he forbore any answer until he had regained his self-possession. Then, with a coolness that surprised even himself, he said -

"That's a broad accusation, Mr. Jasper. Will you go with me to your authority?"

Jasper was not just prepared for a response like this; and he cooled down, instantly, several degrees.

"My authority is quite satisfactory," he returned, still manifesting angry feeling. "That you have been slandering me is plain; and, also, betraying the confidential transactions of the house. It is full time we parted - full time. I didn't dream that I was warming an adder to sting me?"

T. S. Arthur

"I must insist, Mr. Jasper," said Claire firmly, "that you give me your authority for all this. Let me stand face to face with the man who has so broadly accused me."

"Then you deny it all?"

"I shall neither affirm nor deny any thing. You have angrily accused me of having done you a great wrong. All I ask is your authority, and the right to stand face to face with that authority. This is no light matter, Mr. Jasper."

"Well said, young man. It is no light matter, as you will, perhaps, know to your sorrow in the end. Don't suppose, for a moment, that I shall either forget or forgive this outrage. Leave me because I cheat in my business!" An expression of unmitigated contempt was on his face. "Poh! What hypocrisy! I know you! And let Mr. Melleville beware. He, I more than suspect, is at the bottom of this. But he'll rue the day he crossed my path - he will!"

And Jasper ground his teeth in anger.

By this time, Claire had become entirely self-possessed. He was both surprised and troubled; yet concealed, as far as possible, the real state of his feelings.

"So far as Mr. Melleville is concerned," said he, "I wish you to understand, that I applied to *him* for the situation."

"Exactly! That is in agreement with what I heard. I was such a rogue that you could not live with me and keep a clear conscience - so you sought for a place with an honest man."

Claire dropped his eyes to the floor, and stood musing for some considerable time. When he raised them, he looked steadily at his employer and said -

"Mr. Jasper, I never made use of the words you have repeated."

"If not the very words, those of a like signification?"

"To whom? There is no need of concealment, Mr. Jasper." Claire was feeling less and less anxious for the result of this conference every moment. "Speak out freely, and you will find me ready to do the same. There had been some underhand work here - or some betrayal of an ill-advised confidence. The former, I am most ready to believe. In a word, sir, and to bring this at once to an issue - your informant in this matter is Henry Parker, who lives with Mr. Melleville."

The change instantly perceptible in the manner of Jasper showed that Edward's suspicion was right. He had, all at once, remembered that, during his conversation with Melleville, this young man was near.

"I see how it is," he continued. "An eavesdropper has reported, with his own comments and exaggerations, a strictly confidential interview. Such being the case, I will state the plain truth of the matter. Are you prepared to hear it?"

"Oh, certainly," replied Jasper, with a covert sneer in his voice. "I'm prepared to hear any thing."

"Very well. What I have to say is now wrung from me. I did not wish to leave you in anger. I did not wish to draw upon me your ill-will. But, what is unavoidable must be borne. It is true, Mr. Jasper, as you have been informed, that I am not satisfied with your way of doing business."

"How long since, pray?" asked Jasper, with ill-disguised contempt.

"I did not like it in the beginning, but gradually suffered myself to think that all was fair in trade, until I found I was no better than a common cheat! Happily, I have been able to make a sudden pause in the way I was going. From this time, I will serve no man who expects me to overreach a customer in dealing. So soon as my mind was fully made up to leave your employment, I called to see my old friend, Mr. Melleville; stated to him, frankly and fully, what I thought and felt; and asked him if he could not make room for me in his store. Parker doubtless overheard a part of what we were saying, and reported it to you. I would, let me say in passing, much rather hold my relation to this unpleasant business than his. Mr. Melleville offered me my old salary - four hundred dollars - and I agreed to enter his service."

"Four hundred dollars!" Jasper said this in unfeigned surprise.

"Yes, sir; that is all he can afford to pay, and of course all I will receive."

"And I offered you six hundred and fifty."

"True."

"Edward, you are the most consummate fool I ever heard of."

"Time will show that," was the undisturbed reply. "I have made my election thoughtfully, and am prepared to meet the result."

"You'll repent of this; mark my word for it."

"I may regret your ill-will, Mr. Jasper; but never repent this step. I'm only thankful that I possessed sufficient resolution to take it."

"When are you going?"

"Not before the end of this month, unless you wish it otherwise. I would like to give you full time to supply my place."

"You can go at once, if it so please you. In fact, after what has just passed, I don't see how you can remain, or I tolerate your presence."

"I am ready for this, Mr. Jasper," coolly replied the young man.

"How much is due you?" was inquired, after a brief silence.

"Twenty-five dollars, I believe," answered Claire.

Jasper threw open a ledger that lay on the desk, and, turning to the young man's account, ran his eyes up the two columns of figures, and then struck a balance.

"Just twenty-seven dollars," said he, after a second examination of the figures. "And here's the money," he added, as he took some bills from the desk and counted out the sum just mentioned. "Now sign me a receipt in full to date, and that ends the matter."

The receipt was promptly signed.

"And now," sneered Jasper, bowing with mock deference, "I wish you joy of your better place. You will, in all probability, hear from me again. I haven't much faith in your over-righteous people; and will do myself the justice to make some very careful examinations into your doings since you entered my service. If all is right, well; if not, it won't be good for you. I'm not the man to forgive ingratitude, injury, and insult - of all three of which you have been guilty."

"We will not bandy words on that subject, Mr. Jasper," said Claire - "I simply deny that I have been guilty of either of the faults you allege. As for an investigation into my business conduct, that you can do as early and as thoroughly as you please. I shall feel no anxiety for the result."

Jasper did not reply. For a few moments the young man stood as if expecting some remark; none being made, he turned away, gathered together a few articles that were his own private property, tied them into a bundle and marked his name thereon. Then bowing to the merchant, he retired - oppressed from recent painful excitement, yet glad, in his inmost feelings, that a connection so dangerous as that with Jasper had been dissolved - dissolved even at the cost of making an enemy.

CHAPTER IX

As no event of particularly marked interest occurred with those whose histories we are writing, during the next few years, we will pass over that time without a record. Some changes of more or less importance have taken place, in the natural progress of things; but these will become apparent as we pursue the narrative.

A dull, damp November day was losing itself in the sombre twilight, when Edward Claire left the store of Mr. Melleville, and took his way homeward. An errand for his wife led him past his old place of business. As he moved along the street, opposite, he noticed a new sign over the door, the large gilt letters of which were strongly reflected in the light of a gas-lamp. It bore the words, JASPER & PARKER.

Involuntarily the young man sighed. If he had remained with Jasper, there was little doubt but that his name would have been the one now associated with his in a copartnership. Parker was the young man who had betrayed the conversation between Claire and Mr. Melleville. His end in doing this was to gain the favour of Jasper, and thus secure the place left vacant by the departing clerk. He had succeeded in his purpose. Jasper offered him the situation, and he took it. Five years afterward, in which time Jasper had made money rapidly, he was elevated to the position of partner, with a fair interest in the business. He had been honest toward his employer, because he saw that through him there was a chance to rise. Honest in heart he was not, for he never scrupled to overreach

T. S. Arthur

a customer.

Edward Claire, as we have remarked, sighed involuntarily. His own prospects in life were not what are called flattering. His situation with Mr. Melleville was now worth five hundred dollars a year, but his family had increased, and with the increase had come new wants. The condition of Mr. Melleville's business gave him no encouragement to hope for a larger income while in his service. Several times during the last two years he had made application for vacant places, but without success. Sometimes he felt restless and discouraged, as his vision penetrated the future; but there was ever a cheerful light at home that daily dispelled the coming shadows.

Scarcely had the sigh lost itself on the air, when a hand was laid on his arm, and an old acquaintance said -

"Ah, Edward! How are you?"

Claire seeing the face of his friend, returned the greeting cordially.

"What have you been doing with yourself?" asked the latter. "It is months, I believe, since I had the pleasure of meeting you."

"Busy all day," returned Clare, "and anchored at home in the evening. So the time is passing."

"Pleasantly and profitably, I hope," said the friend.

"Pleasantly enough, I will own," was answered; "as to the profit - if you mean in a money sense - there is not much to boast of."

"You are still with Melleville?"

"Yes."

"At what salary?"

"Five hundred."

"Is that all? How much family have you?"

"Three children; or, I might say four; but the fourth brings us three hundred dollars a year for her maintenance."

"That is something."

"Oh yes. It is quite a help."

"By the way, Edward - the new store we just past reminds me of it - your old friend Jasper has just given one of his clerks, named Parker, an interest in his business."

"So I am aware."

"Jasper is doing first-rate."

"He is making money, I believe."

"Coining it. The fact is, Edward, you never should have left him. Had you kept that situation, you would have been the partner now. And, by the way, there was rather a strange story afloat at the time you took it into your head to leave Jasper."

"Ah! what was it?"

"It is said that you thought him a little too close in his dealings, and left him on that account. I hadn't given you credit for quite so tender a conscience. How was it, Edward?"

"I didn't like his modes of doing business, and, therefore, left him. So far you heard truly."

"But what had you to do with *his* modes of doing business?"

"A great deal. As one of his employees, I was expected to carry out his views."

"And not being willing to do that, you left his service."

"That is the simple story."

"Excuse me, Edward, but I can't help calling you a great fool. Just see how you have stood in your own light. But for this extra bit of virtue, for which no one thinks a whit the better of you, you might this day have been on the road to fortune, instead of Parker."

"I would rather be in my own position than in his," replied Claire firmly.

"You would!" His companion evinced surprise. "He is in the sure road to wealth."

"But not, I fear, in the way to happiness."

"How can you say that, Edward?"

"No man, who, in the eager pursuit of money, so far forgets the rights of others as to trample on them, can be in the way to happiness."

"Then you think he tramples on the rights of others?"

"I know but little, if any thing, about him," replied Claire; "but this I do know, that unless Leonard Jasper be a different man from what he was five years ago, fair dealing between man and man is a virtue in a clerk that would in nowise recommend him to the position of an associate in business. His partner must be shrewd, sharp, and unscrupulous - a lover of money above every thing else - a man determined to rise, no matter who is trampled down or destroyed in the ascent."

"In business circles such men are by no means scarce."

"I am aware of it."

"And it is unhesitatingly affirmed by many whom I know, that, as the world now is, no really honest man can trade successfully."

"That is more than I am ready to admit."

"The sharpest and shrewdest get on the best."

"Because it is easier to be sharp and shrewd than to be intelligent, persevering, industrious, patient, and self-denying. The eagerness to get rich fast is the bane of trade. I am quite ready to admit that no man can get rich at railroad speed, and not violate the law of doing as you would be done by."

"Doing as you would be done by! O dear!" said the friend; "you certainly don't mean to bring that law down into the actual life of the world?"

"It would be a happier world for all of us if this law were universally obeyed."

"That may be. But, where all are selfish, how is it possible to act from an unselfish principle?"

"Do you approve of stealing?" said Claire, with some abruptness.

"Of course not," was the half-indignant answer.

"I need not have asked the question, for I now remember to have seen the fact noticed in one of our papers, that an unfaithful domestic in your family had been handed over to the police."

"True. She was a thief. We found in her trunk a number of valuable articles that she had stolen from us."

"And you did right. You owed this summary justice as well to the purloiner as to the public. Now, there are many ways of stealing, besides this direct mode. If I deprive you of your property with design, I steal from you. Isn't that clear?"

"Certainly."

"And I am, to use plain words, a thief. Well, now take this easily to be understood case. I have a lot of goods to sell, and you wish to purchase them. In the trade I manage to get from you, through direct misrepresentation, or in a tacit advantage of your ignorance, more than the goods are really worth. Do I not cheat you?"

"Undoubtedly."

"And having purposely deprived you of a portion of your money, am I not a thief?"

"In all that goes to make up the morality of the case, you are."

"The truth, unquestionably. Need I proceed further? By your own admission, every businessman who takes undue advantage of another in dealing, steals."

"Pretty close cutting, that, friend Claire. It wouldn't do to talk that right out at all times and in all places."

"Why not?"

"I rather think it would make some people feel bad; and others regard themselves as insulted."

"I can believe so. But we are only talking this between ourselves. And now I come back to my rather abrupt question - Do you approve of stealing? No, you say, as a matter of course. And yet, you but just now were inclined to justify sharp dealing, on the ground that all were sharpers - quoting the saying of some, that no honest man could trade successfully in the present time. For the direct stealing of a few articles of trifling value, you hand a poor, ignorant domestic over to the police, yet feel no righteous indignation against the better-taught man of business, who daily robs his customers in some one form or another."

"You are too serious by far, Edward," returned his companion, forcing a laugh. "Your mind has fallen into a morbid state. But you will get over this one of these times. Good evening! Our ways part here. Good evening!"

And the young man turned off abruptly.

"A morbid state," mused Claire to himself, as he continued on alone. "So thousands would say. But is it so? Is honesty or dishonesty the morbid state? How direct a question! How plain the answer! Honesty is health - dishonesty the soul's sickness. To be honest, is to live in obedience to social and divine laws; dishonesty is the violation of these. Is it possible for a diseased body to give physical enjoyment? No! Nor can a diseased mind give true mental enjoyment. To seek happiness in the possession of wealth obtained through wrong to the neighbour, is as fruitless as to seek bodily pleasure in those practices which inevitably destroy the health. To me, this is self-evident, and may God give me strength to live according to my clear convictions!"

The very earnestness with which Claire mentally confirmed himself in his honest convictions, and especially his upward looking for strength in conscious weakness, showed that his mind was in temptation. He had felt somewhat depressed during the day, in view of his external relation to the world; and this feeling was increased by his observation of the fact that Parker had been advanced to the position of a partner to his old employer. It seemed like a reward for unfair dealing, while honesty was suffered to remain poor. The young man's enlightened reason - enlightened during five years' earnest search after and practice of higher truths than govern in the world's practice - strongly combated all the false arguments that were presented to his mind, during this season of his overshadowing. The combat was severe, and still continued on his arrival at home - causing his mind to be in a measure depressed.

CHAPTER X

The increase of Claire's family had caused him, some time before, to remove from the two comfortable rooms in which were passed the first pleasant years of his married life. He now occupied a small house in a retired street, the rent of which, though moderate, drew pretty heavily on his income. But he had managed, through the prudent co-operation of his wife, not only to keep even with the world, but to lay by a small sum of money.

Few homes, in the large city wherein dwelt this obscure family, were so full of all the elements of happiness. If, sometimes, the spirit of Claire was overshadowed by passing clouds - as would unavoidably happen from his contact with the world, and his own variant states - the evening's return to the bosom of his family, generally made all bright again.

Little Fanny Elder, now ten years of age, had been steadily growing into his affections from the first. It is questionable whether his love for his own children was a purer passion. Older, by several years, than Edith, she had been to him more companionable; and had ever greeted his return at evening with warmer expressions of pleasure than were manifested by Edith, or the two younger children who had been added to the number of his household treasures.

On this evening, as Claire drew nearer and nearer to his home, and his thoughts began to make pictures of the scene within, its light and warmth penetrated his feelings, and when he

T. S. Arthur

opened, at length, the door, he was himself again.

First to bound into his arms was Fanny Elder. What a beautiful, fairy-like creature she was! How more than fulfilled the promise of her early childhood! Next came Edith, now six years of age, side by side with her brother Harry, a wild little rogue, and were only a few seconds behind Fanny in throwing themselves upon their father; while little baby Mary, as she sat on the carpet, fluttered her tiny arms, and crowed out her joyous welcome.

What a merry romp they all had for the next two or three minutes. When quiet came back again, baby was sitting on one knee, Harry on the other, and Fanny leaning her face on the shoulder of her "father" - for so she called him with the rest - while her glossy curls were resting in sunny clusters upon his bosom. The memory of the child's former home and parents seemed to have faded almost entirely. If the past ever came back to her, like a dream, with its mingled web of sunshine and tears, she never spoke of it. Fully had she been taken into the hearts and home of her now parents; and she rested there as one having a right to her position.

And the pure spirit who presided over this little Paradise, where was she? Present - observing all, and sharing in the delight her husband's return had occasioned. The expected kiss had not long been kept from her loving lips.

Happy household! What have its inmates to envy in those around them? Within the circle of many squares were none so rich in all the elements of happiness.

Soon after the evening meal was over, the children, after another merry romp with their father, went off to bed. When Mrs. Claire returned from the chamber, whither she had accompanied them, she held a letter in her hand.

"I had forgotten all about this letter, Edward," said she. "It was left here for you, this afternoon."

Claire took the letter and broke the seal, running his eye down to the signature as he unfolded it.

"Leonard Jasper! What is this?"

His brow contracted instantly, as he commenced reading the letter. It was brief, and in these words -

"MR. EDWARD CLAIRE - *Sir*: From this time I relieve you of the burden of my ward, Fanny Elder. Mrs. Jasper and myself have determined to take her into our own family, in order that we may give the needful care to her education. Call around and see me to-morrow, and we will arrange this matter. Yours, &c. LEONARD JASPER."

The face of the young man had become pale by the time he had finished reading this letter; but that of his wife, who did not yet know a word of its contents, was almost white - the effect produced on her husband filling her with a vague alarm.

"What is it, Edward?" she asked, in a low, eager whisper.

"Jasper wants us to give up Fanny."

Edith sank into a chair, exclaiming -

"Oh, Edward!"

"But she is only ten years of age," said the husband, "and our contract is to keep her until she is twelve."

"We cannot give her up," murmured Edith, tears already beginning to flow over her cheeks. "I never thought of this. What can it mean?"

"Some sudden determination on the part of Jasper, and based on nothing good," was the reply. "But, as I said, our contract is binding until Fanny is twelve years of age, and I will never consent to its being broken. He was over anxious to hold me in writing. He did not value his own word, and would not trust mine. It was well. The dear child shall remain where she is."

"But, after she is twelve, Edward? What then? Oh, I can never part with her," said Mrs. Claire, now weeping freely.

"Two years will pass ere that time. Jasper may have other purposes in view when our present contract expires."

"You will see him in the morning?"

"O yes. I must understand all about this matter. What can it mean? 'Needful care to her education!' A mere hypocritical pretence. What does he care for her, or her education? What, in fact, does he know of her? Nothing at all. Has he ever called to see her? Has he ever made the first inquiry after her? No. There is something wrong, without doubt. This movement bodes no good to our dear child. But she has one friend who will stand between her and harm - who will protect her, if need be, at the risk of his own life."

Claire, as his words indicate, had suffered himself to become much excited. Seeing this, his wife recovered, to some extent, her own self-possession, and spoke to him soothingly.

"We will wait and see what it means," said she. "Mr. Jasper cannot force her away from us now, if he would."

"After seeing him to-morrow, you can understand better what we are to expect. This note may have been written from some momentary feeling. I cannot think that he has a settled purpose to take the child from us."

"Time will show," was the abstracted response.

Not for years had so unhappy an evening been spent by Edward Claire and his wife; and when they retired, it was to pass the night in broken intervals of sleep.

Early on the next morning, Claire called at the store of Jasper, who received him with cold politeness, and at once came to the matter uppermost in both their thoughts, by saying -

"You received my note?"

"I did," was the reply.

"Well? All right, I suppose?"

"Fanny is not twelve years of age yet!"

"Isn't she? Well, what of that?" There was some impatience in the manner of Jasper.

"I agreed to take the care of her until she was twelve."

"Well - well - suppose you did? I'm her guardian, and wish to have her now in my own family. If you agreed to keep her, I did not say that she should positively remain."

"There was a contract signed to that effect," firmly replied Claire.

"A contract! Humph! Are you sure?"

"Very sure. You drew it yourself."

"Have you a copy of it?"

"I have."

Jasper seemed thrown aback by this. He had not forgotten the contract, for all his affected ignorance thereof. He only hoped that Edward had, through carelessness, lost his copy. But he was mistaken.

"A contract! A contract?" said Jasper, as if communing with his own thoughts. "I do remember, now, something of the kind.

T. S. Arthur

And so there was a written contract?"

"Yes, sir; and I have a copy in your own hand."

"And I am to understand, Edward, that notwithstanding my wish, as the child's legal guardian, and, therefore, the representative of her parents, to have her in my own family, that you will interpose a hasty-signed contract?"

"Mr. Jasper," said the young man, changing his manner, "we have had this child in our family for over five years, and have grown strongly attached to her. In fact, she seems to us as one of our own children; and we, to her, are in the place of parents. To remove her would, therefore, be doing a great violence to our feelings, and I know it would make her unhappy. Let her remain where she is, and you may rest assured that she will be cared for as tenderly as our own."

"No, Edward, it is no use to talk of that," replied Jasper, positively. "I wish, now, to have her in my own family, and trust that you will not stand for a moment in the way."

"But, Mr. Jasper" -

"It will be of no avail to argue the point, Edward," said the merchant, interrupting him. "I was fully in earnest when I wrote to you, and am no less in earnest now. I am certainly entitled to the possession of my ward, and will not bear, patiently, any attempt on your part to deprive me of that right."

There was an angry quivering of the lips, and a stern knitting of the brows, on the part of Jasper, as he closed this emphatic sentence. Claire felt excited, yet was so fully conscious of the necessity of self-control, that he quieted down his feelings, and endeavoured to think calmly.

"Well, what do you say?" imperatively demanded Jasper, after waiting some moments for a reply.

"We cannot part with the child," said the young man, in a low, appealing voice.

"You *must* part with her!" was the quick, resolute response.

"Must? That is a strong word, Mr. Jasper." Claire's manner underwent another change, as was shown by the firm compression of his lips, and the steady gaze of his eyes, as he fixed them on the merchant.

"I know it is strong, but no stronger than my purpose; and I warn you not to stand in my way. I've got an old grudge against you, so don't provoke me too far in this matter. A pretty affair, indeed, when *you* attempt to come between me and my legal rights and duties."

"Duties!" There was a stinging contempt in the young man's voice. The manner of Jasper had chafed him beyond all manner of self-control.

"You forget to whom you are speaking," said the latter, offended now, as well as angry. "But we will not bandy words. Will you, without further trouble, give into my hands the child of Mr. Elder?"

"I cannot do it, Mr. Jasper."

"Speak positively. Will you, or will you not do as I wish?"

"I will not," was the decided answer.

"Enough." And Jasper turned away, muttering in an undertone, "We'll soon see who is to be master here."

Claire lingered a short time, but, as Jasper showed no disposition to renew the conversation, he left the store, greatly disturbed and troubled in his mind.

CHAPTER XI

When Edward Claire and his wife drew together on the evening of that day, after the children were in bed, both were calmer than at their previous interview on a subject that necessarily brought with it strong excitement of feeling. Both had thought much and felt much, and were now prepared to look calmly at the new relation affairs had so suddenly assumed. At dinner-time, Edward had related the substance of his interview with Jasper.

"What can he do?" asked Edith, referring now to the muttered threat of that individual.

"I don't know that he can do any thing more than withhold the regular sums heretofore paid for the support of Fanny. If he does that, I will collect them legally."

"Can't he take her away by force? Won't the law compel us to give her up?" asked Edith, in a troubled voice.

"Our contract gives us a right to her possession until she is twelve years of age. In that, the law will undoubtedly sustain us."

"The law is very uncertain, Edward."

"But our contract is plainly worded, and, in this State, private written contracts between parties to an agreement are good in law. At best, however, we can only keep her two years longer;

that is what troubles me most."

"We must do our duty by her," said Edith, endeavouring to speak calmly, "during that time; and wean our hearts from her as much as possible, so that the giving of her up, when it has to be done, will cause as little grief as possible. Poor child! It will be hard for her to leave us, and go to her new home. That thought is beginning to pain me most."

"And such a home! I have seen Mrs. Jasper frequently, and, if my observation is correct, she is no true woman. Dress, it seemed to me, was all she cared for; and there was a captiousness and ill-temper about her, at times, that was, to say the least of it, very unbecoming."

"And to her care we must resign this precious one," said Edith, with a sigh. "Oh, how the thought pains me! Dear, dear child!"

"The time is yet distant," remarked Claire - "distant by nearly two years. Let it be our duty to prepare her as fully for the new relation as possible. Two years is a long time - many changes will take place, and among them, it may be, a change in the purpose of Mr. Jasper. We will hope for this, at least; yet wisely prepare for a different result."

"As things now appear, I do not see what else remains for us to do. Ah me! How like lightning from a summer sky has this flashed suddenly over us. But, Edward, we must not, in the strong trial of our natural feelings, permit ourselves to forget that dear Fanny is in the higher guardianship of One who is infinitely wise and good. If she is to pass from our care to that of Mr. Jasper and his family, it is through His permission, and He will bring out of it good to all."

"I can see that in my understanding, Edith," replied her husband; "but, it is hard to *feel* that it is so."

"Very hard, Edward. Yet, it is something - a great deal - to have the truth to lean upon, even though it seems to bend under our weight. Oh! without this truth, it seems as if I would now fall to the ground helpless. But, let us try and view this painful subject in its brightest aspect. It is our duty to the child to keep her, if we can, until she passes her twelfth year."

"Clearly," replied the husband.

"And you think we can do so?"

"We have two advantages - possession and a written contract guaranteeing the possession."

"True."

"These on our side, I think we have little to fear from Jasper. The great trial will come afterward."

To this conclusion, that is, to retain Fanny until her twelfth year, if possible - they came, after once more carefully reviewing the whole subject; and, resting here, they patiently awaited the result.

With what a new interest was the child regarded from this time! How the hearts of Claire and his wife melted toward her on all occasions! She seemed to grow, daily, more and more into their affections; and, what to them appeared strange - it might only have been imagination - manifested a more clinging tenderness, as if conscious of the real truth.

Weeks elapsed and nothing further was heard from Jasper. Claire and his wife began to hope that he would make no attempt to separate Fanny from them; at least not until her twelfth year. Let us turn to him, and see what he is doing, or proposing to do, in the case.

Two or three days subsequent to the time when Claire received the notification from Jasper, just referred to, two men sat, in close conference, in the office of an attorney noted for his legal intelligence, but more noted for his entire want of principle.

For a good fee, he would undertake any case, and gain for his client, if possible, no matter how great the wrong that was done. His name was Grind. The two men here introduced, were this lawyer and Jasper.

"Do you really think," said the latter, "that, in the face of my guardianship, he can retain possession of the child?"

"He has, you say, a copy of this contract?" Grind held a sheet of paper in his hand.

"Yes. To think that I was such a fool as to bind myself in this way! But I did not dream, for a moment, that things were going to turn up as they have."

"It is a contract that binds you both," said the lawyer, "and I do not see that you can go round it."

"I must go round it!" replied Jasper, warmly. "You know all the quirks and windings of the law, and I look to you for help in this matter. The possession of that child, is, to me, a thing of the first importance."

"After two years she will come into your hands without trouble, Mr. Jasper. Why not wait?"

"Wait! I will not hear the word. No! no! I must have her now."

"The law will not give her to you, Mr. Jasper," returned Grind, with the utmost self-possession. "The contract is clearly expressed; and it is binding."

"Is there no way to accomplish my end?" said Jasper, impatiently. "There must be. I cannot be foiled in this matter. Even pride would forbid this. But, there are stronger motives than pride at work now."

"Can you allege ill-treatment against the young man or his wife? Or neglect of your ward's comfort? Have they failed to

T. S. Arthur

do their duty by her in any respect?"

"I should not wonder; but, unfortunately, I can prove nothing."

"You might call for an investigation."

"And if every thing was proved right on their part?"

"The court would, most probably, return the child to their care. I am ready to take all necessary steps for you; but, Mr. Jasper, I very strongly incline to the opinion that the least noise you make in this matter, the better. Couldn't you - for a consideration in money, for instance - overcome the reluctance of Claire and his wife to part with the child? Honey, you know, catches more flies than vinegar."

"Buy him off, you mean?"

"Yes."

"No - no! I hate him too cordially for that. He's a villain in disguise; that's my opinion of him. A low, canting hypocrite. Buy him off for money. Oh no!"

"Could he be bought?" asked the lawyer.

"Could he?" A flush of surprise lit up, for a moment, the face of Jasper. "What a question for *you* to ask. Hasn't every man his price? Bought! Yes, I could buy him fifty times over."

"Then do so, and in the quietest manner. That is my advice."

"I'll steal the child!" exclaimed Jasper, rising up in his excitement, and moving uneasily about the room.

Grind shook his head, as he replied -

"All folly. No man ever did a wise thing while he was in a

passion. You must permit yourself to cool down a great many degrees before you can act judiciously in this matter."

"But to be thwarted by him!" An expression of the deepest disgust was in the face of Jasper.

"All very annoying, of course," was the response of Grind. "Still, where we can't make things bend exactly to our wishes, it is generally the wisest policy to bend a little ourselves. We often, in this way, gain a purchase that enables us to bring all over to our side."

It must not be supposed that Grind, in giving his client advice that was to prevent an appeal to law, did so from any unselfish friendliness. Nothing of the kind. He saw a great deal to gain, beyond; and, in his advice, regarded his own interests quite as much as he did those of Jasper. He was not, however, at this interview, able to induce the merchant to attempt to settle the matter with Claire by compromise. The most he could do was to get him to promise, that, for the present, he would make no effort to get the person of the child into his possession.

Jasper, when he left his lawyer, was less satisfied with him than he had ever been. In previous cases, he had found Grind ready to prosecute or defend, and to promise him the fullest success - though success did not always come.

Several more consultations were held during the succeeding two or three weeks, and, finally, Jasper was brought over fully to his lawyer's way of thinking.

T. S. Arthur

CHAPTER XII

The minds of Claire and his wife were yet in a state of suspense, when, some weeks after the first interview, the former received a politely worded note from Jasper, requesting him to call at his store. He went, accordingly, and Jasper received him with marked suavity and kindness of manner, and, after making a few inquiries about his family, said -

"Edward: I believe I must confess to having been a little over-excited at our last interview. The fact is, I had forgotten all about that contract; and when you brought it to my mind so abruptly, I was thrown somewhat off of my guard, and said things for which I have since felt regret. So let what is past go. I now wish to have another talk with you about Fanny Elder. How is the child?"

"She is very well."

"And she has grown, I presume, finely?"

"Yes. She's now quite a stout girl."

"What kind of a child is she? Docile and obedient?"

"None could be more so. A sweeter disposition I have never seen."

"How are you getting on now, Edward?" Mr. Jasper's voice was kind and insinuating.

"Comfortably," was answered.

"What is your salary?"

There was a momentary hesitation on the part of Claire, and then he replied -

"Five hundred dollars."

"Is that all? I was under the impression that you received a thousand. I am very certain that some one told me so. Too little, Edward - too little. You are worth more than that to any one. Are you acquainted at Edgar & Co.'s?"

"No."

"I wish you were. One of their young men is going to leave, and they will have to fill his place immediately. The salary is twelve hundred."

Claire's heart gave a quick bound.

"Shall I speak to Edgar for you?" added the merchant.

"If you will do so, Mr. Jasper," said Edward, with a sudden earnestness of manner, "I shall be greatly indebted to you. I find it a little difficult to get along on five hundred dollars a year."

"How much family have you now?"

"Three children."

"Indeed. Oh yes, you should have a higher salary. I know you would just suit Edgar & Co., and I think the place may be secured for you."

A few moments of silence followed, and then Jasper resumed -

T. S. Arthur

"But, as just said, I wish to talk with you about this ward of mine. Your salary is so light that you, no doubt, find the income received through her quite a help to you?"

"No - no," replied Claire; "it costs for her boarding, clothes, schooling, etc., quite as much as we receive."

"It does?" Jasper manifested some surprise.

"Oh yes. We have no wish to make any profit out of her."

"That being the case, Edward," said the merchant, "why are you so reluctant to give her up?"

"Because," was the reply, "both myself and wife have become strongly attached to her. In fact, she seems like one of our own children."

"When she is twelve, you know," Edward, returned Jasper, "you will have to resign her. Our agreement only extends to that time." He spoke in a mild, insinuating, friendly tone of voice. So much so, in fact, that Claire, well as he knew him, was partially deceived and thrown off of his guard.

"True; unless you have seen reason by that time, which we hope will be the case, to let her remain in her present home. Believe me, Mr. Jasper," - Claire spoke earnestly - "that Fanny will take the parting very hard, if ever it comes."

"As come it must, Edward, sooner or later," was the mild, yet firm response.

"Are you so earnest about this, Mr. Jasper? I have flattered myself that you did not really care a great deal about having Fanny."

"I am entirely in earnest, Edward," was the reply. "I may have seemed to you indifferent about this child, but such has not been the case. I have feelings and purposes in regard to her which I cannot explain, but which are near my heart. I see your position and that of your wife, and I feel for you. If compatible with what I conceive to be my duty, I would let her remain under your care. But such is not the case. Surely, it will be far better for both you and Fanny for the change that must come to be made now."

The calm, kind, insinuating manner of Jasper disarmed Claire, and made him wish that he could meet the desire of his old employer, without the painful breach in his home circle which must be the consequence. With his eyes cast upon the floor, he sat silently communing with his own thoughts for some time. The announcement of a vacancy in the house of Edgar & Co., and the offer to try and get the situation for him, had flattered his mind considerably. If he did not make some compromise in the present case, he could count nothing on the influence of Jasper. But, how could he compromise? There was but one way - to give up Fanny - and that he was not prepared to do.

Seeing that the young man remained silent, Jasper said -

"Edward, I will make you this very liberal offer. Understand, now, that I am deeply in earnest - that the possession of Fanny is a thing of great moment to me; and that to gain this desired object, I am prepared to go very far. If you will meet me in a spirit of compromise, I will become as I was some years ago, your friend; and I have the ability to aid any one materially. As just said, I will make you this liberal offer: - Let me have the child now, and for the next two years I will pay you the same that you have been receiving for her maintenance."

Claire lifted his head quickly. There was already a flush on his cheeks and a sharp light in his eyes.

"Stay - one moment," interrupted Jasper, who saw by the motion of his lips that he was about replying. "I will pay you the whole sum, six hundred dollars, in advance, and, in addition thereto, pledge myself to procure for you, within three mouths, a situation worth a thousand dollars per annum, at least."

This was too broad an attempt to buy over the young man, and it failed. Starting to his feet, with a feeling of indignation in his heart so strong that he could not repress it, he answered, with knit brows and eyes fixed sternly and steadily on the merchant - "Leonard Jasper! I thought you knew me better! I am not to be bought with your money."

As sudden was the change that passed over the merchant. He, too, sprang to his feet, and conscious that his offer of bribery, which he had humiliated himself to make, had failed, with clenched hand and set teeth, he fairly hissed out -

"You'll rue this day and hour, Edward Claire - rue it even to the moment of death! I will never forget nor forgive the wrong and insult. Don't think to escape me - don't think to foil me. The child is mine by right, and I will have her, come what will."

Feeling how useless it would be to multiply words, Claire turned away and left the store. He did not go home immediately, as he had thought of doing, in order to relieve the suspense of his wife, who was, he knew, very anxious to learn for what purpose Jasper had sent for him; but went to his place of business and laid the whole substance of his interview before his fast friend, Mr. Melleville, whose first response was one of indignation at the offer made by Jasper to buy him over to his wishes with money. He then said -

"There is something wrong here, depend upon it. Was there much property left by the child's parents?"

"Two houses in the city."

"Was that all?"

"All, I believe, of any value. There was a tract of land some-where in the State, taken for debt; but it was considered of little account."

"Regard for the child has nothing to do with this movement," remarked Mr. Melleville. "The character of Jasper precludes the supposition."

"Entirely. What can it mean? The thing comes on me so suddenly that I am bewildered."

Claire was distressed.

"You are still firm in your purpose to keep Fanny until she is twelve years old?"

"As firm as ever, Mr. Melleville. I love the child too well to give her up. If a higher good to her were to be secured, then I might yield - then it would be my duty to yield. But, now, every just and humane consideration calls on me to abide by my purpose - and there I will abide."

"In my mind you are fully justified," was the reply of Mr. Melleville. "Keep me fully advised of every thing that occurs, and I will aid you as far as lies in my power. To-day I will call upon Edgar & Co., and do what I can toward securing for you the place said by Jasper to be vacant. I presume that I have quite as much influence in this quarter as he has."

CHAPTER XIII

Scarcely had Edward Claire left the store of Jasper, ere the latter went out hurriedly, and took his way to the office of Grind, the lawyer, to whom he said, as he entered -

"It's just as I feared. The miserable wretch proved as intractable as iron." Jasper was not only strongly excited, but showed, in his voice and manner, that he had suffered no ordinary disappointment.

"Couldn't you buy him over?" There was a mixture of surprise and incredulity in the lawyer's tones.

"No," was the emphatic response.

"That's strange! He's poor?"

"He gets five hundred a year, and has a wife and three children to support."

"Why didn't you tempt him with the offer to get him a place worth a thousand?"

"I did."

"With what effect?"

"He wouldn't give up the child."

"Humph!"

"Isn't it too bad, that a mean-souled fellow like him should stand in our way at such a point of time? I could spurn him with my foot! Hah!"

And Jasper clenched his teeth and scowled malignantly.

"I am disappointed, I confess", said Grind. "But angry excitement never helped a cause, good or bad. We must have possession of this child somehow. Martin came down from Reading this morning. I saw him but an hour ago."

"Indeed! What does he say?"

"The indications of coal are abundant. He made very careful examinations at a great number of points. In several places he found it cropping out freely; and the quality, as far as he was able to judge, is remarkably good."

"Will he keep our secret?" said Jasper.

"It is his interest to do so."

"We must make it his interest, in any event. No time is now to be lost."

"I agree with you there. A single week's delay may ruin every thing. The coal is our discovery, and we are, in all equity, entitled to the benefit."

"Of course we are. It's a matter of speculation, at best; the lucky win. If we can get an order for the sale, we shall win handsomely. But, without producing the child, it will be next to impossible to get the order. So we must have her, by fair means or by foul."

"We must," said the lawyer, compressing his lips firmly.

T. S. Arthur

"And have her now."

"Now," responded Grind.

Jasper rose to his feet.

"It's easy enough to say what we must have," remarked Grind, "but the means of gaining our ends are not always at hand. What do you propose doing?"

"I shall get the child."

"Don't act too precipitately. Violence will excite suspicion, and suspicion is a wonderful questioner."

"We must play a desperate game, as things now are, or not play at all," said Jasper.

"True; but the more desperate the game, the more need of coolness, forethought, and circumspection. Don't forget this. How do you mean to proceed?"

"That is yet to be determined."

"Will you make another effort to influence Claire?"

"No."

"Do you regard him as altogether impracticable?"

"No influence that I can bring would move him."

"You will, then, resort to stratagem or force?"

"One or the other - perhaps both. The child we must have."

"Let me beg of you, Jasper, to be prudent. There is a great deal at stake."

"I know there is; and the risk increases with every moment of delay."

Grind showed a marked degree of anxiety.

"If the child were in our possession now," said Jasper, "or, which is the same, could be produced when wanted, how soon might an order for the sale be procured?"

"In two or three weeks, I think," replied the lawyer.

"Certain preliminary steps are necessary?"

"Yes."

"If these were entered upon forthwith, how soon would the child be wanted?"

"In about ten days."

"Very well. Begin the work at once. When the child is needed, I will see that she is forthcoming. Trust me for that. I never was foiled yet in any thing that I set about accomplishing, and I will not suffer myself to be foiled here."

With this understanding, Jasper and the lawyer parted.

A week or more passed, during which time Claire heard nothing from the guardian of Fanny; and both he and his wife began to hope that no further attempt to get her into his possession would be made, until the child had reached her twelfth year.

It was in the summer-time, and Mrs. Claire sat, late in the afternoon of a pleasant day, at one of the front-windows of her dwelling, holding her youngest child in her arms.

"The children are late in coming home from school," said she, speaking aloud her thought. "I wonder what keeps them!"

And she leaned out of the window, and looked for some time earnestly down the street.

But the children were not in sight. For some five or ten minutes Mrs. Claire played with and talked to the child in her arms; then she bent from the window again, gazing first up and then down the street.

"That's Edie, as I live!" she exclaimed. "But where is Fanny?"

As she uttered this inquiry, a sudden fear fell like a heavy weight on her heart. Retiring from the window, she hastened to the door, where, by this time, a lady stood holding little Edie by the hand. The child's eyes were red with weeping.

"Is this your little girl?" asked the lady.

"Oh, mamma! mamma!" cried Edie, bursting into tears, as she sprang to her mother's side and hid her face in her garments.

"Where did you find her, ma'am? Was she lost?" asked Mrs. Claire, looking surprised as well as alarmed. "Won't you walk in, ma'am?" she added, before there was time for a reply.

The lady entered, on this invitation, and when seated in Mrs. Claire's little parlour, related that while walking through Washington Square, she noticed the child she had brought home, crying bitterly. On asking her as to the cause of her distress, she said that she wanted Fanny: and then ran away to some distance along the walks, searching for her lost companion. The lady's interest being excited, she followed and persuaded the child to tell her where she lived. After remaining some time longer in the square, vainly searching for Fanny, she was induced to let the lady take her home. After hearing this relation, Mrs. Claire said to Edith, in as calm a voice as she could assume, in order that the child might think without the confusion of mind consequent upon excitement -

"Where is Fanny, dear?"

"She went with the lady to buy some candies," replied the child.

"What lady?" asked the mother.

"The lady who took us to the square."

"The lady who took you to the square?" said the mother, repeating the child's words from the very surprise they occasioned.

"Yes, mamma," was the simple response.

"What lady was it?"

"I don't know. She met us as we were coming home from school, and asked us to go down and walk in the square. She knew Fanny."

"How do you know, dear?" disked Mrs. Claire.

"Oh, she called her Fanny; and said what a nice big girl she was growing to be."

"And so you went down to the square with her?"

"Yes, ma'am."

"And what then?"

"We walked about there for a little while, and then the lady told me to wait while she took Fanny to the candy-store to buy some candy. I waited, and waited ever so long; but she didn't come back; and then I cried."

The meaning of all this, poor Mrs. Claire understood but too well. With what a shock it fell upon her. She asked no further question. What need was there? Edie's artless story made every thing clear. Fanny had been enticed away by some one

T. S. Arthur

employed by Jasper, and was now in his possession! With pale face and quivering lips, she sat bending over Edie, silent for several moments. Then recollecting herself, she said to the lady -

"I thank you, ma'am, most sincerely, for the trouble you have taken in bringing home my little girl. This is a most distressing affair. The other child has, evidently, been enticed away."

"You will take immediate steps for her recovery," said the lady.

"Oh, yes. I expect my husband home, now, every moment."

While she was yet speaking, Claire came in. Seeing the white face of his wife, he exclaimed -

"Mercy, Edith! What has happened?"

Edith could only murmur the word "Fanny," as she started forward, and buried her face, sobbing, on his bosom.

"Fanny! What of her? Oh, Edith! speak!"

The agitation of the wife was, for the time, too overpowering to admit of words, and so Claire turned to the lady and said, hurriedly -

"Will you tell me, madam, what has happened?"

"It appears, sir," she replied, "that a strange lady enticed the children to Washington Square, on their way from school" -

"And then carried off our dear, dear Fanny!" sobbed out Edith.

"Carried off Fanny!" exclaimed Claire.

"This lady," said Edith, growing calmer, "found our little Edie crying, in the square, and brought her home. Edie says the lady took them down there, and then told her to wait until she went with Fanny to buy some candies. They went, but did not return."

The meaning of all this was quite as clear to the mind of Edward Claire as it was to his wife. He understood, likewise, that this was the work of Jasper, and that Fanny was now in his possession. What was to be done?

"Our first step," said Claire, after the stranger had retired, "must be to ascertain, if possible, whether what we believe to be true in regard to Fanny is really true. We must know certainly, whether she be really in the hands of Mr. Jasper."

"Where else can she be?" asked Edith, a new fear throwing its quick flash into her face.

"We, naturally," replied her husband, "take it for granted that Mr. Jasper has put his threat into execution. There is a bare possibility that such is not the case; and we must not rest until we have, on this point, the most absolute certainty."

"For what other purpose could she have been enticed away?" said Mrs. Claire, her face again blanching to a deadly paleness.

"We know nothing certain, Edith; and while this is the case, we cannot but feel a double anxiety. But, I must not linger here. Be as calm as possible, my dear wife, in this painful trial. I will go at once to Mr. Jasper, and learn from him whether he has the child."

"Go quickly, Edward," said Edith. "Oh! it will be such a relief to have a certainty; to know even that she is in his hands."

Without further remark, Claire left his house and hurried off to the store of Jasper. The merchant was not there. From one of his clerks he learned his present residence, which happened not to be far distant. Thither he went, and, on asking to see him, was told by the servant that he was not at home. He then inquired for Mrs. Jasper, who, on being summoned, met him in one of the parlours. The manner of Claire was very much agitated, and he said, with an abruptness that evidently disconcerted the lady -

"Good evening, madam! My name is Claire. You remember me, of course?"

The lady bowed coldly, and with a frown on her brow.

"Is little Fanny Elder here?" was asked, and with even greater abruptness.

"Fanny Elder? No! Why do you ask that question?"

There was something so positive in the denial of Mrs. Jasper, that Claire felt her words as truth.

"Not here?" said he, catching his breath in a gasping manner. "Not here?"

"I said that she was not here," was the reply.

"Oh, where then is she, madam?" exclaimed the young man, evincing great distress.

"How should I know? Is she not in your possession? What is the meaning of this, Mr. Claire?"

The lady spoke sternly, and with the air of one both offended and irritated.

"Somebody enticed her away, on her return from school this afternoon," said Claire. "Mr. Jasper said that he would have her; and my first and natural conclusion was that he had executed his threat. Oh, ma'am, if this be so, tell me, that my anxiety for the child's safety may have rest. As it is, I am in the most painful uncertainty. If she is here, I will feel, at least" -

"Have I not told you that she is not here, and that I know

nothing of her," said Mrs. Jasper, angrily, interrupting the young man. "This is insolent."

"How soon do you expect Mr. Jasper home?" inquired Claire.

"Not for several days," replied Mrs. Jasper.

"Days! Is he not in the city?"

"No, sir. He left town yesterday."

Claire struck his hands together in disappointment and grief. This confirmed to him the lady's assertion that she knew nothing of Fanny. In that assertion she had uttered the truth.

Sadly disappointed, and in far deeper distress of mind than when he entered the house, Edward Claire retired. If Mr. Jasper left the city on the day previous, and his wife had, as he could not help believing, no knowledge whatever of Fanny, then the more distressing inference was that she had been enticed away by some stranger.

On his way home, Claire called again at the store of Jasper. It occurred to him to ask there as to his absence from the city. The reply he received was in agreement with Mrs. Jasper's assertion. He had left town on the previous day.

"Where has he gone?" he inquired.

"To Reading, I believe," was the answer.

"Will he return soon?"

"Not for several days, I believe."

With a heavy heart, Claire bent his way homeward. He cherished a faint hope that Fanny might have returned. The hope was vain. Here he lingered but a short time. His next step was to give information to the police, and to furnish for all the morning papers an advertisement, detailing the circumstances attendant on the child's abduction. This done, he again returned home, to console, the best he could, his afflicted wife, and to wait the developments of the succeeding day.

Utterly fruitless were all the means used by Claire to gain intelligence of the missing child. Two days went by, yet not the least clue to the mystery of her absence had been found. There was no response to the newspaper advertisements; and the police confessed themselves entirely at fault.

Exhausted by sleepless anxiety, broken in spirit by this distressing affliction, and almost despairing in regard to the absent one, Mr. And Mrs. Claire were seated alone, about an hour after dark on the evening of the third day, when the noise of rumbling wheels ceased before their door. Each bent an ear, involuntarily, to listen, and each started with an exclamation, as the bell rang with a sudden jerk. Almost simultaneously, the noise of wheels was again heard, and a carriage rolled rapidly away. Two or three quick bounds brought Claire to the door, which he threw open.

"Fanny!" he instantly exclaimed; and in the next moment the child was in his arms, clinging to him, and weeping for joy at her return.

With a wonderful calmness, Mrs. Claire received Fanny from her husband, murmuring as she did so, in a subdued, yet deeply gratified voice -

"O, God! I thank thee!"

But this calmness in a little while gave way, and her over-strained, but now joyful feelings, poured themselves forth in tears.

Poor child! She too had suffered during these three never-to-be-forgotten days, and the marks of that suffering were sadly visible in her pale, grief-touched countenance.

To the earnest inquiries of her foster-parents, Fanny could give no very satisfactory answer. She had no sooner left the square with the lady mentioned by little Edith, than she was hurried into a carriage, and driven off to the cars, where a man met them. This man, she said, spoke kindly to her, showed her his watch, and told her if she would be a good girl and not cry, he would take her home again. In the cars, they rode for a long time, until it grew dark; and still she said the cars kept going. After a while she fell asleep, and when she awoke it was morning, and she was lying on a bed. The same lady was with her, and, speaking kindly, told her not to be frightened - that nobody would hurt her, and that she should go home in a day or two.

"But I did nothing but cry," said the child, in her own simple way, as she related her story. "Then the lady scolded me, until I was frightened, and tried to keep back the tears all I could. But they would run down my cheeks. A good while after breakfast," continued Fanny, "the man who had met us at the cars came in with another man. They talked with the lady for a good while, looking at me as they spoke. Then they all came around me, and one of the men said -

"'Don't be frightened, my little dear. No one will do you any harm; and if you will be a right good girl, and do just as we want you to do, you shall go home to-morrow.'

"I tried not to cry, but the tears came running down my face. Then the other man said sharply -

"'Come now, my little lady, we can't have any more of this! If you wish to go home again tomorrow, dry your tears at once. There! there! Hush all them sobs. No one is going to do you any harm.'

"I was so frightened at the way the man looked and talked, that I stopped crying at once.

"'There!' said he, 'that is something like. Now,' speaking to the lady, 'put on her things. It is time she was there.'

"I was more frightened at this, and the men saw it; so one of them told me not to be alarmed, that they were only going to show me a large, handsome house, and would then bring me right back; and that in the morning, if I would go with them now, and be a good girl, I should go home again.

"So I went with them, and tried my best not to cry. They brought me into a large house, and there were a good many men inside. The men all looked at me, and I was so frightened! Then they talked together, and one of them kept pointing toward me. At last I was taken back to the house, where I stayed all day and all night with the lady. This morning we got into the cars, and came back to the city. The lady took me to a large house in Walnut street, where I stayed until after dark, and then she brought me home in a carriage."

Such was the child's story; and greatly puzzled were Claire and his wife to comprehend its meaning. Their joy at her return was intense. She seemed almost as if restored to them from the dead. But, for what purpose had she been carried off; and who were the parties engaged in the act? These were questions of the deepest moment; yet difficult, if not impossible of solution - at least in the present. That Jasper's absence from the city was in some way connected with this business, Claire felt certain, the more he reflected thereon. But, that Fanny should be returned to him so speedily, if Jasper had been concerned in her temporary abduction, was something that he could not clearly understand. And it was a long time ere the mystery was entirely unravelled.

CHAPTER XIV

From that time Claire and his wife heard no more from Jasper, who regularly paid the sums quarterly demanded for Fanny's maintenance. This demand was not now made in person by Claire. He sent a written order, which the guardian never failed to honour on the first presentation.

Mr. Melleville, according to promise, called upon the firm of Edgar & Co., in order to speak a good word for Edward; but learned, not a little to his surprise, that no vacancy was anticipated in the house.

"Mr. Jasper," said he, "told one of my young men that a clerk had left, or was about leaving you."

"It's a mistake," was the positive answer. "He may have meant some other firm."

"All a wicked deception on the part of Jasper," said Melleville to himself, as he left the store. "A lie told with sinister purpose. How given over to all baseness is the man!"

Claire was no little disappointed when this was told him; but his answer showed how he was gaining in just views of life; and how he could lean on right principles and find in them a firm support.

"I would rather," said he, "be the deceived than the deceiver. The one most wronged in this is Leonard Jasper. Ah! is he not preparing for himself a sad future? As for me, I am more and more satisfied, every day, that all events, even to the most minute, are in the direction or permission of Providence; and that out of the very occurrences we deem afflictive and disastrous, will often arise our greatest good. For the moment I was disappointed; but now I feel that it is all right."

No change of marked importance occurred in the family of Claire during the next two years, to the close of which period both he and his wife looked with increasing earnestness of mind. Fanny had grown rapidly during this time, and was now tall for her age - and still very beautiful. In character she was every thing the fondest parents could desire.

At last came the child's twelfth birthday. Neither Clare nor his wife referred to the fact; though it was present to both their minds - present like an evil guest. Must they now give her up? Their hearts shrank and trembled at the bare idea. How plainly each read in the other's face the trouble which only the lips concealed!

Never had Fanny looked so lovely in the eyes of Claire as she did on that morning, when she bounded to his side and claimed a parting kiss, ere he left for his daily round of business. Could he give her up? The thought choked in their utterance the words of love that were on his lips, and he turned from her and left the house.

As Claire, on his way to Mr. Melleville's store, came into the more business portions of the city, his thoughts on the child who was soon to be resigned, according to the tenor of his contract with her guardian, he was suddenly startled by seeing Jasper a short distance ahead, approaching from the direction in which he was going. Happening, at the moment, to be near a cross street, he turned off suddenly, in obedience to an instinct rather than a purpose, and avoided a meeting by going out of his way.

"How vain," he sighed to himself, as the throbbing of his heart grew less heavy and his thoughts ran clear. "I cannot so avoid this evil. It will most surely find me out. Dear, dear child! How shall we ever bear the parting!"

All day long Claire was in momentary dread of a visit or a communication from Jasper. But none came. A like anxiety had been suffered by his wife, and it showed itself in the pallor of her cheeks, and the heavy, almost tearful, drooping of her eyelids.

The next day and the next passed, and yet nothing was heard from the guardian. Now, the true guardians of the child began to breathe more freely. A week elapsed, and all remained as before. Another week was added; another and another. A month had gone by. And yet the days of a succeeding month came and went, the child still remaining in her old home.

Up to this time but brief allusions had been made by either Claire or his wife to the subject first in their thoughts. They avoided it, because each felt that the other would confirm, rather than allay, fears already too well defined.

"It is strange," said Claire, as he sat alone with his wife one evening, some three months subsequent to the twelfth birthday of Fanny, "that we have heard nothing yet from Mr. Jasper."

Edith looked up quickly, and with a glance of inquiry, into his face; but made no answer.

"I've turned it over in my mind a great deal," resumed Claire, thoughtfully; "but with little or no satisfactory result. Once I thought I would call on him" -

"Oh, no, no! not for the world!" instantly exclaimed Edith.

"I see, with you, dear, that such a step would be imprudent. And, yet, this suspense - how painful it is!"

"Painful, it is true, Edward; yet, how in every way to be

T. S. Arthur

preferred to the certainty we so much dread."

"O yes - yes. I agree with you there." Then, after a pause, he said, "It is now three months since the time expired for which we agreed to keep Fanny."

"I know," was the sighing response.

They both remained silent, each waiting for the other to speak. The same thought was in the mind of each. Excited by the close pressure of want upon their income, Edward was first to give it voice.

"Mr. Jasper," said he, touching the subject at first remotely, "may have forgotten, in the pressure of business on his attention, the fact that Fanny is now twelve years old."

"So I have thought," replied Edith.

"If I send, as usual, for the sum heretofore regularly paid for her maintenance, it may bring this fact to his mind."

"I have feared as much," was the low, half-tremulous response.

"And yet, if I do not send, the very omission may excite a question, and produce the consequences we fear."

"True, Edward. All that has passed through my mind over and over again."

"What had we better do?"

"Ah!" sighed Edith, "if we only knew that."

"Shall I send the order, as usual?"

Edith shook her head, saying -

"I'm afraid."

"And I hesitate with the same fear."

"And yet, Edith," said Claire, who, as the provider for the family, pondered more anxiously the question of ways and means, "what are we to do? Our income, with Fanny's board added, is but just sufficient. Take away three hundred dollars a year, and where will we stand? The thought presses like a leaden weight on my feelings. Debt, or severe privation, is inevitable. If, with eight hundred dollars, we only come out even at the end of each year, what will be the result if our income is suddenly reduced to five hundred?"

"Let us do what is right, Edward," said his wife, laying her hand upon his arm, and looking into his face in her earnest, peculiar way. Her voice, though it slightly trembled, had in it a tone of confidence, which, with the words she had spoken, gave to the wavering heart of Claire an instant feeling of strength.

"But what is right, Edith?" he asked.

"We know not now," was her reply, "but, if we earnestly desire to do right, true perceptions will be given."

"A beautiful faith; but oh, how hard to realize!"

"No, Edward, not so very hard. We have never found it so: have we?"

Love and holy confidence were in her eyes.

"We have had some dark seasons, Edith," said Claire sadly.

"But, through darkest clouds has come the sunbeam. Our feet have not wandered for want of light. Look back for a moment. How dark all seemed when the question of leaving Jasper's service came up for decision. And yet how clear a light shone when the time for action came. Have you ever regretted what was then done, Edward?"

"Not in a sane moment," replied the young man. "O no, no, Edith!" speaking more earnestly; "that, with one exception, was the most important act of my life."

"With one exception?" Edith spoke in a tone of inquiry.

"Yes." Claire's voice was very tender, and touched with a slight unsteadiness. "The *most* important act of my life was" -

He paused and gazed lovingly into the face of his wife. She, now comprehending him, laid, with a pure thrill of joy pervading her bosom, her cheek to his - and thus, for the space of nearly a minute, they sat motionless.

"May God bless you, Edith!" said Claire at length, fervently, lifting his head as he spoke. "You are the good angel sent to go with me through life. Ah! but for you, how far from the true path might my feet have strayed! And now," he added, more calmly, "we will look at the present difficulty steadily, and seek to know the right."

"The right way," said Edith, after she had to some extent repressed the glad pulses that leaped to her husband's loving words, "is not always the way in which we most desire to walk. Thorns, sometimes, are at its entrance. But it grows pleasanter afterward."

"If we can find the right way, Edith, we will walk in it because it is the right way."

"And we will surely find it if we seek in this spirit," returned the wife.

"What, then, had we best do?" asked Claire, his thought turning earnestly to the subject under consideration.

"What will be best for Fanny? That should be our first consideration," said his wife. "Will it be best for her to remain with us, or to go into Mr. Jasper's family?"

"That is certainly a grave question," returned Claire, seriously, "and must be viewed in many aspects. Mr. Jasper's place in the world is far different from mine. He is a wealthy merchant; I am a poor clerk. If she goes into his family, she will have advantages not to be found with us - advantages of education, society, and position in life. To keep her with us will debar her from all these. Taking this view of the case, Edith, I don't know that we have any right to keep her longer, particularly as Mr. Jasper has signified to us, distinctly, his wish, as her guardian, to take her into his own family, and superintend her education."

Edith bent her head, thoughtfully, for some moments. She then said -

"Do you believe that Mr. Jasper gave the true reason for wishing to have Fanny?"

"That he might superintend her education?"

"Yes."

"No, Edith, I do not. I believe a selfish motive alone influenced him."

"You have good reasons for so thinking?"

"The best of reasons. I need not repeat them; they are as familiar to you as they are to me."

"Do you believe that, under his superintendence, she will receive a better education than under ours?"

"She will, undoubtedly, Edith, if remaining with us she fails to bring the means of education. We are poor, Edith, and the claims of our own children - bone of our bone and flesh of our flesh - must not be forgotten."

A quick change passed over Edith. Her countenance became

troubled. The difficulties in the way of retaining the child were suddenly magnified to her thoughts. Ah! how painfully did she feel that often the first steps in the way of duty are among thorns.

"Can we be just to Fanny and just also to our own children?" asked Claire.

"If we still received the old sum for her maintenance, we could. I would not ask its increase to the amount of a single dollar."

"Nor I, Edith. Were we certain of having this continued, there would be no doubt."

"There would be none in my mind. As for the higher position in society which she would attain, as an inmate of Mr. Jasper's family, that might not be to her the greatest good; but prove the most direful evil. She could not be guarded there, in her entrance into life, as we would guard her. The same love would not surround her as a protecting sphere. I tremble at the thought, Edward. How great would be her danger! Fourfold would be her temptation, and tenfold her exposure."

"We will keep her," said Claire, firmly, as his wife ceased speaking. "She must not be so exposed. God has given her to us; she is our child, for we love her as tenderly as if she were of our own blood. When her mother was taken, God transferred the love she had borne her child into your bosom, and from that time you became her mother. No, Edith, we must not let her go forth, in her tender innocence. We love her as our own; let us share with her the best we have; let her become more really our own than she has yet been."

"If," said Edith, after some moments, "we lose the regular income from Mr. Jasper, Fanny will be deprived of most important advantages. Just now we are about adding materially to the cost of her education."

"I know," replied Edward. "But if the income is withheld?"

"We have not yet applied for it."

Claire looked, for some moments, steadily into his wife's face.

"You think, then, that we should make the usual application?"

"I have not said so, Edward. My mind is far from clear. Jasper may not, now, want the trouble of Fanny. He doubtless had some purpose to subserve when he demanded her; a purpose gained, probably, at the time of her mysterious removal from the city, which I have always believed was through his agency. If you were to send for the money, as usual, it is more than probable that he would pay it."

"But, if he should refuse, and demand the child?"

"If his purpose to do this remains, and he has forgotten Fanny's age, your omission to send for the money will be more likely to call his thought to the subject, than your regular demand for the price of her maintenance."

"True."

"And if he still means to have her, the execution of his purpose cannot in any event be long delayed."

"No."

"Can *we* unaided give her the education she is entitled to receive?"

Claire shook his head.

"Then had we not better continue to apply for the sum necessary to her support and education. If Mr. Jasper is indifferent about her, the money will be paid as usual; if he means to take her into his own family, our failure to apply will defer but for a very short season the evil day."

Edith's mind had become clear by this time. Her husband not making an immediate reply, she added -

"This acting on mere policy, is never, I think, the wisest. Does it not clearly involve a distrust in Providence, and a weak reliance on mere human prudence? There is a provision for Fanny's support and education, and she is justly entitled to all those natural advantages which this provision was designed to give. Under Providence, Mr. Jasper has been chosen her guardian; and under Providence the personal care of the child has fallen to our lot. Thus far we have endeavoured to discharge our duty faithfully - thus far we have done as well by the child as if she had been our own. Now, if it is best for her to remain with us, the same Providence will so dispose of events as to provide for her remaining; but if it is best for her to go into the family of Mr. Jasper, she will go there. Let us not, therefore, in our practical distrust of Providence, seek to hide ourselves from the observation of a mere creature."

"I see much in this," said Claire, as soon as his wife had ceased speaking. "Man proposes; God disposes. With Him are all our ways. Out of the evil designs and selfish purposes of men, He is ever bringing forth good."

"Then let us not fear to trust him. As we have been doing, let us continue to do, confidently believing that He will overrule all for good. To our present sight, it seems, that, unless we receive, as heretofore, a sum of money for Fanny's support and education, we cannot do for her what is right. This, at least, is my view."

"And it is mine," replied the husband.

"Then let us act from the light we have. None can do better than this."

And so it was determined to send an order to Jasper, as usual.

CHAPTER XV

On the next day, a fellow-clerk, who had always performed this little service for Claire, took the order to Jasper. With a nervous impatience that he found it impossible to repress, Claire awaited his return. On his appearance, he said, with ill-concealed anxiety -

"Did he pay the order?"

The young man shook his head.

"What! Didn't pay it?" Though half-expecting such a result, he was none the more prepared for it, nor the less disturbed when it was known.

"No; he said that the contract entered into with you for boarding the child was at an end three months ago."

"What else did he say?"

"Nothing else."

"Did he send no message to me of any kind?"

"None. When I handed him the order, he pushed it back, and used the words I have repeated. I waited a little while for some further remark, but he made none."

"Did he seem angry?"

T. S. Arthur

"Not angry; but rather pleased, I should say. There was a heartless smile on his face, as if he enjoyed the act of refusal."

Claire made no further remark. For a time he groped about, mentally, like one in darkness and lost. It appeared as if there was no escape; as if the evil which had long dogged his steps was upon him. But in a short time, a ray of light shone in here and there, paths that might be walked in safely were dimly perceived - escape seemed possible. Still, he was deeply depressed and sorely troubled.

Edith received the intelligence in a calmer spirit than her husband had expected.

"The way will be made plain before us," said she. "It is plainer now than it was last night - much plainer."

"How can you say that, Edith?"

"Mr. Jasper has refused to pay any thing more to us for Fanny's support."

"Yes."

"But in the refusal said nothing about our giving her up to him."

"Well?"

"I gather from this, and the fact that he was aware of her being twelve years old, that he does not really want her now in his own family, but refuses to pay us for her board and education from a feeling of ill-will toward you. His manner to the young man who presented the order clearly indicates this."

"You may be right there, Edith," said Claire, a further light breaking into his mind. "We have at least done our duty toward Fanny in making this demand on her guardian. And now, the question left for us to decide may be whether it will be just toward her, and also toward our own children, still to keep her in our own family, and let her share, with the others, the best that it is in our power to give."

"And will it be hard to make that decision?" said Edith, a slight flush coming into her earnest face.

"I think not," was the firm reply.

"Have we loved her less than our own?" asked Edith.

"I believe not."

"Love seeks the highest good for its object."

"Yes - yes."

"Can a stranger love the child as we have loved her?"

Claire shook his head.

"Can a stranger, even with more of what the world gives, yet with less of a genuine affection, secure for her, as we may, what should justly be regarded as the highest good in life."

"No stranger can ever be to her, Edith, what you have been, and will continue to be."

"We must not thrust her out, Edward. We cannot thrust her out. While God permits her to remain, let us keep her, assured that He will send for her use all things needful."

"Most cheerfully will I prolong my daily toil for her sake," replied Claire; "and cheerfully will I make sacrifice of personal comfort. Yes, let her remain where she is, so long as, in God's providence, she is permitted to remain. If Jasper continues to withhold the price of her maintenance, there will be the more left for her when she becomes of age; and then, if there are defects in her education, a few years of earnest application on

T. S. Arthur

her part, will remove them. Even now, we could compel him to pay for her a reasonable sum, but in securing this, we would assuredly lose the child, for this man's anger would burn hot against us."

"I have thought of that," replied Edith. "No, our only plain course, for the present, is to look away from Jasper, and regard Fanny as one of our own children."

To this conclusion the mind of Claire and his wife came firmly. Then the painful agitation they had for some time suffered gradually subsided, and they began earnestly to cast about for the ways and means whereby so large an extra draft as was likely to be made upon their slender income could be met.

Two propositions were made by Edith: one was, that they should make a reduction in their expenses, by moving into a smaller house. They now paid two hundred dollars annually for rent; and she was sure that, for one hundred and fifty, they might suit themselves very well. The other proposition was, to give two or three hours every evening, after the children were in bed, to fine needle-work, in which she was well skilled.

"I could easily earn two dollars a week, in this way," was her confident remark.

Claire, who had other plans in his mind, did not speak very encouragingly of these propositions, though he avoided disapproval. Increased expense demanded an increase of income; and his thoughts were all now bent suggestively in that direction. As for Edith, her burdens were heavy enough; and her husband, though he did not check her generous enthusiasm, by no means acquiesced in the plan of evening toil for his wife out of the range of her many domestic duties.

A few days went by, with no incident of importance. Claire, during the time, appeared, to his wife more thoughtful that usual. One evening he came home with a brighter countenance.

"Good news, Edie," said he in a cheerful voice, as soon as the children's glad and noisy welcome of their father was over; and he drew his wife aside as he spoke.

"Good news, dear," he repeated. "I was sure the way would open for us, and it has opened."

"How, Edward?" asked Edith, with a quickly flushing face. "How has it opened?"

"I've secured employment for my evenings, at six dollars a week. So all will go on with us the same as usual. The only drawback lies in the fact that you will have to remain at home alone. But, for the sake of the end, you will bear that cheerfully."

The light which had come into Edith's countenance faded.

"What kind of employment?" she inquired, with a slight huskiness of voice.

"I've engaged to act as clerk in an auction store, where they have regular night-sales."

Edith shook her head.

"I thought you would be so delighted," said her husband, evidently much disappointed.

"You often come home, now, overwearied with the day's labour," replied Edith.

"An hour at tea-time will refresh me for the evening's work. Don't think of that a moment, Edith."

"How can I help thinking of it? No, no, Edward, you must not do this. It will destroy your health. You are not very strong."

"My health is perfectly good, Edith."

But Edith shook her head -

"Not so very good. You look paler, and are much thinner than you were a year ago. A little over-exertion throws your system off of its balance; and then you are sick."

"I will be very careful of myself," replied Claire. "If, after a few weeks, the extra labour is found to be too severe, I can give up the place. Nothing like trying, you know, dear."

Still, Edith was not satisfied. Very strongly she urged her husband not to increase his labour in the degree contemplated.

"Let us try if we can reduce our expenses by a closer economy. It is better to deny ourselves things not necessary to health, than to injure health by extra labour."

She urged this view, however, in vain. Claire could not, without at least a trial of his strength, decline the important offer which had been made to him. And so, after a consultation with Mr. Melleville, he entered upon his new employment, leaving his wife to spend the hours of his absence alone. Not idly were those hours spent. What she had at first proposed to do, she now began to execute. Without saying any thing to her husband, she had procured, from a friend who kept a fancy-store, and who took in from the ladies a great deal of work, some fine sewing; and with this she was busily occupied until his return, which did not take place on the first night until near eleven o'clock.

There was a slight drawback in the pleasure both felt in meeting at this late hour - the drawback of weariness. Yet their hearts were tranquil and elevated in the consciousness that they were denying self for the good of another - and that one most tenderly beloved. Again the way had become plain before them; and if strength only were given to bear their increased burdens, they would move on with even lighter footsteps than before.

And now, after having lingered thus long with the humble clerk, let us turn to the rich merchant; for Jasper has become a man of extensive possessions. Wealth flowed in upon him with extraordinary rapidity - not in the regular course of trade, overreaching and unscrupulous as he was in dealing, but through what are called fortunate speculations. How he made his first hundred thousand dollars - the basis of his present very large fortune - was not clearly understood, though sundry vague rumours on the subject were afloat, none of them, however, very near the truth, except in the admission that a fraud on somebody had been committed. But let us introduce Mr. Jasper.

On the night that Claire entered upon his duties as clerk in the auction store, and about the same hour that his duties began, Mr. Jasper, who was walking restlessly the floor of his richly furnished parlours, his mind busy with some large money-making scheme, yet fretted by a recent disappointment, found himself suddenly in the presence of, to him, a well-known individual, whose ring at the door he had not observed.

"Martin!" he exclaimed, in no affected surprise. "Is it possible?"

"Ah, Jasper! How are you? Right glad to get sight of your face again!" said the other familiarly, as he grasped the merchant's passive hand, and squeezed it until the joints cracked.

"When did you arrive in the city?" returned Jasper, as he reached his visitor a chair. He did not speak with much warmth; and yet there was an effort to be at ease and cordial.

"Some two hours ago," said Martin, in whose face was already beginning to gather a few lines in token of the sober thoughts that lay beneath his assumed smiling exterior.

"From which direction did you come?"

"West. I'm from the Upper Mississippi."

T. S. Arthur

"Ah!"

"I went to Galena some five or six months ago; and have since been actively engaged in lead-mining. A great business that, Mr. Jasper."

"Ah?" This "ah?" was particularly chilling.

"There are more rapid fortunes made at the lead-mines in the neighbourhood of Galena, at present, than in any part of the United States," said Martin, approaching, by rapid advances, the subject nearest to his thoughts.

"You think so?" returned Jasper, with cold incredulity.

"I know so," was the positive response. "I could point you to a dozen men who have made their tens of thousands annually for the last five or ten years."

"It is easy to talk about making tens of thousands, Martin; but the fact itself is a more difficult matter."

"A fact is a fact, however, Mr. Jasper," said the other. "What is done, is done."

"Of course."

"It is a fact that money is made at the lead-mines, hand over fist," continued Martin. "Of this I am prepared to give you the strongest kind of evidence."

"Why should you be so anxious to convince me of this fact?" returned the merchant. "I have quite as many irons in the fire now as I can see to."

"Ah! That may be," said Martin, forcing to his rather hard features a bland smile. "But these new irons I will keep from burning."

"It's no use, Martin, to talk of lead-mines to me," said Jasper firmly. "I am spread out enough already. Contraction, not expansion, is my present motto. I've met with more than one heavy loss since I saw you."

"Have you, indeed? I'm sorry for that. But a false card will turn up now and then, you know. The game in the long run is sure."

"We're sure of nothing," replied Jasper, with considerable feeling.

"I wouldn't like to say that. Of course, all plans will not succeed; for man's judgment is far from possessing the virtue of infallibility. But human reason would be a poor endowment, did it not lead us, in most cases, to right conclusions, if we are careful in our modes of using this high faculty."

"The purpose of your visit to the East," said Jasper, who understood perfectly the man with whom he was dealing, and, therefore, determined to know at once the length and breadth of what he was expected to do, "is, I presume, to enlist some capitalists here in a lead-mining speculation?"

"My ideas do not extend quite that far," was Martin's answer. "Too many cooks, you are aware, sometimes spoil the broth. To come to the point at once, let me explain the purpose of my present journey to the East."

"Well; I am all attention."

"My fur-trade business, as I wrote you a year ago, turned out disastrously."

"Yes."

"After that, I opened a small store in one of the frontier towns, and I did very well, all things considered. But the gain was too

T. S. Arthur

slow to suit my ideas of things; so, meeting with a fair chance, I sold out, and bought a lead-mine, which I have been working ever since to good profit. Recently, I struck upon one of the richest veins ever discovered. If properly worked, it will yield a rapid fortune. But I have not sufficient capital to avail myself of the advantages offered, and have come on here to lay the matter before you, and to offer you a share in the business."

Jasper shook his head, saying -

"I have more business on my hands now, Martin, than I can possibly attend to."

"You don't know what you are declining, Mr. Jasper," urged Martin warmly. "You havn't yet looked at the statements which I am prepared to lay before you."

"I do know one thing," was the feeling answer, "and that is, that I am declining trouble and cost. About that part of the business, there can be little question."

"Then," said Martin, his manner changing, "I am to understand that you do not wish to join me in this matter?"

"Yes. I would like you to understand that distinctly."

"Very well. I am sorry you refuse so advantageous an investment of money; for right sure am I that no other investment you can make will turn out as this would have done. But, as you have declined, I will not offer a share in my good fortune to any one else; but prosecute the work to my own advantage."

"I thought you hadn't the capital to do that," said Jasper, speaking with ill-repressed eagerness.

"Nor have I," coolly answered Martin. "The proposition I was about to make was this - an advance of twenty thousand dollars capital on your part, to constitute you an equal partner in the mine. But this you decline."

"Certainly! certainly! I would not have entertained it for a moment."

"Exactly. So I have already inferred. I will, therefore, as just said, retain this advantage in my own hands. But, Mr. Jasper, I shall need some help."

The visitor fixed his eyes keenly on the merchant as he said this. There was a momentary pause. Then he resumed.

"I shall only want about ten thousand dollars, though; and this you must obtain for me."

"Martin! Do you think I am made of money?" exclaimed Jasper, starting to his feet, and facing his companion, in the attitude and with the expression of a man who, finding himself in the presence of an enemy, assumes the defensive.

"Oh no," was the quiet answer - "not *made* of money. But, for a particular friend, you can no doubt, easily raise such a trifle as ten thousand dollars?"

"Trifle! You mock me, sir!"

"Don't get excited about this matter, Mr. Jasper," coolly returned Martin, whose name the reader has probably recognised as that of an agent employed by the merchant and Grind, the lawyer, some years before, in making investigations relative to the existence of coal on certain lands not far from Reading, Pennsylvania. "Don't get excited," he repeated. "That will do no good. I have not come to rob you. I don't ask you to give me ten thousand dollars. All I want is a loan, for which I will pledge good security."

"What kind of security?" asked Jasper quickly.

"Security on my lead-mine."

T. S. Arthur

"Pooh! I wouldn't give the snap of a finger for such security!"

Jasper, thrown off his guard, spoke more contemptuously than was prudent.

An instant change was visible in Martin, who, rising, commenced buttoning up his coat. There was about him every mark of a man deeply offended.

"Good evening, sir!" said he, with a low, formal bow, yet with his eyes fixed searchingly in those of the merchant.

"Martin," - Jasper did not smile, nor was there in his voice the slightest affectation of good feeling - yet his manner and tone were both decisive, - "Martin, sit down again. Talk in reason, and I will hear."

The man resumed his seat, and, with his eyes still in those of Jasper, said -

"I have talked in reason. You are worth, so report says, not less than three hundred thousand dollars. How the first hundred thousand came, is known, certainly, only to one man beside you and me. In procuring that large sum I was a very prominent agent."

"You have already been paid for your services a dozen times over."

"There may be a difference of opinion about this," replied the man boldly - "and there *is* a difference of opinion."

"I have already advanced you over five thousand dollars."

"What of that! Five thousand to three hundred thousand that you have made by the operation."

"You are in error, Martin," said Jasper, with a blended look of perplexity and distress. "I am not worth the sum you have mentioned - nothing like it. My losses during the past six months have been very heavy."

"It is your interest to say this. I can credit as much of it as I please."

"You are insulting! You presume on the power a knowledge of my affairs has given you. I will look for a more honourable agent the next time."

"Honourable! Ha! ha!" The visitor laughed in a low, guttural voice.

"Martin! I will not hear this from any living man."

The face of Jasper was almost purple with suppressed anger.

"Go!" he added. "Leave my house instantly. I defy you!"

Scarcely had these words passed his lips, ere Martin glided from the drawing-room, and in a few moments the street-door shut with a heavy, reverberating jar.

The merchant stood, like one bewildered, for a few moments, and then, as he sank into a chair, uttered a low groan. For a long time he remained as motionless as if sleeping.

CHAPTER XVI

On leaving the house of Jasper, Martin - who, instead of having been in the city only a few hours, arrived two days previously - took his way to the office of Grind, the lawyer. He had seen this individual already several times, and now called on him again by appointment. The two men, on meeting, exchanged looks of intelligence.

"Did you see him?" asked the lawyer, as Martin took a proffered chair.

"I saw him," was replied.

"Can you make any thing out of him?'

"I think so. He fights a little hard; but the odds are against him."

"How much did you ask him to loan you?"

"Ten thousand?"

"Martin! That's cutting a little too sharp."

"Not a hit. He'll never miss such a trifle."

"You can't bleed him that deep," said the lawyer.

"Can't I? You'll see; I could get twenty thousand. But I'm

disposed to be generous. Ten thousand I must and will have."

And the man laughed in a low, self-satisfied, sinister chuckle.

"He's able enough," remarked Grind.

"So you have told me. And if he is able, he must pay. I helped him to a fortune, and it is but fair that he should help me a little, now that a fortune is in my grasp. I only want the money as a loan."

"Wouldn't five thousand answer your purpose?" asked the lawyer. "That is a large sum. It is not a very easy matter for even a rich man, who is engaged heavily in business, to lay down ten thousand dollars at call."

"Five thousand will not do, Mr. Grind."

"Jasper has lost, to my certain knowledge, twenty thousand dollars in three months."

"So much?"

"At least that sum. Money came in so fast, that he grew a little wild in his speculations, and played his cards with the dashing boldness of a gambler while in a run of luck. I cautioned him, but to no good purpose. One of his latest movements had been to put fifty or sixty thousand dollars in a cotton factory?"

"Poh! What folly."

"A most egregious blunder. But he fancies himself an exceedingly shrewd man."

"He has been remarkably fortunate in his operations."

"So he has. But he is more indebted, I think, to good luck than to a sound judgment. He has gone up to dizzy height so rapidly, that his weak head is already beginning to swim."

"What has become of that pretty little ward of his?" asked Martin, somewhat abruptly.

"Why didn't you put that question to him?" replied Grind. "You would have been more likely to get a satisfactory answer."

"I may do so after I have the ten thousand dollars in my pocket. That was rather a shameful business, though; wasn't it? I never had a very tender conscience, but I must own to having suffered a few twinges for my part in the transaction. He received over a hundred thousand dollars for the land?"

"Yes; and that clear of some heavy fees that you and I claimed for services rendered."

"Humph! I'm not quite paid yet. But, touching the child, Mr. Grind: don't you know any thing about her?"

"Nothing, personally."

"What was it Jasper paid for the tract of land?"

"One thousand dollars."

"Paid it into his own hands as the child's guardian."

"Yes; that was the simple transaction."

"Has the public never made a guess at the real truth of this matter?"

"Never, so far as my knowledge goes. There have been some vague whisperings - but no one has seemed to comprehend the matter."

"The purchase was made in your name, was it not?"

"Yes."

"That is, you bought from Jasper as the child's guardian; and afterward sold it back to him."

"Yes."

"Why didn't you hold on to it when it was fairly in your hands? I only wish I had been in your place?"

The lawyer shrugged his shoulders, but did not commit himself by acknowledging that he had, more than once, regretted his omission to claim the property while legally in his hands, and defy Jasper to wrest it from him.

Leaving these two men, whose relation to Jasper is sufficiently apparent to the reader's mind, we will return to the merchant, whom we left half-stupefied at the bold demand of an associate in wrong-doing. A long time passed ere his activity of mind returned. While he sat, brooding - dreamily - over what had just passed, a little daughter came into the parlour, and seeing him, came prattling merrily to his side. But in attempting to clamber upon his knee, she was pushed away rudely, and with angry words. For a few moments she stood looking at him, her little breast rising and falling rapidly; then she turned off, and went slowly, and with a grieving heart, from the room.

Jasper sighed heavily as the child passed out of sight; and rising up, began moving about with a slow pace, his eyes cast upon the floor. The more he dwelt upon the visit of Martin - whom, in his heart, he had wished dead - the more uneasy he felt, and the more he regretted having let him depart in anger. He would give twice ten thousand dollars rather than meet the exposure which this man could make.

Riches was the god of Leonard Jasper. Alas! how little power was there in riches to make his heart happy. Wealth beyond what he had hoped to obtain in a whole lifetime of devotion to mammon, had flowed in upon him in two or three short years. But, was he a happier man? Did he enjoy life with a keener zest? Was his sleep sweeter? Ah, no! In all that went to make up the true pleasure of life, the humble clerk, driven to prolonged hours of labour, beyond what his strength could well bear, through his ill-nature and injustice, was far the richer man. And his wealth consisted not alone in the possession of a clear conscience and a sustaining trust in Providence. There was the love of many hearts to bless him. In real household treasures few were as rich as he.

But, in home treasures, how poor was Leonard Jasper! Poor to the extreme of indigence! The love of his children, reaching toward him spontaneously its tendrils, he rejected in the selfish devotion of every thought and feeling to business as a means of acquiring wealth. And as to the true riches, which many around him were laying up where no moth could corrupt nor thieves break through and steal, he rejected them as of no account.

With such a man as Leonard Jasper, holding the position of head of a family, how little of the true home spirit, so full of tenderness and mutual love, is to be expected! Had Mrs. Jasper been less a woman of the world; had she been capable of loving any thing out of herself, and, therefore, of loving her husband and children, with that true love which seeks their higher good, a different state of things would have existed in this family, spite of Jasper's unfeeling sordidness. But, as it was, no fire of love melted the natural perverseness inherited by the children, and they grew up, cherishing mutual antagonism, and gradually coming to regard their parents only as persons with power to thwart their inclinations, or as possessing the means of gratifying their desires.

With all his wealth, how few were the real sources of happiness possessed by Jasper! Pressed down with anxiety about the future, and forced to toil beyond his strength, how many of life's truest blessings were poured into the lap of Edward Claire!

The sleep of the poor clerk, that night, was sound and refreshing. The merchant tossed to and fro on his pillow until long after the midnight watches advanced upon the morning; and then, when wearied nature claimed her due, he slept only for brief periods, continually startled by frightful dreams.

At an early hour next day, he called upon Grind, who was still his legal adviser.

"Have you seen Martin?" he asked the moment he entered the office.

"Martin! Surely he is not in the city!" returned Grind evasively.

"He surely is," said Jasper, fretfully.

"Martin. Where in the world did he come from? I thought him somewhere in the neighbourhood of the Rocky Mountains. What does he want?

"No good, of course."

"That may be said safely. Have you seen him?"

"Yes."

"When? This morning?"

"No; he called at my house last night."

"Called last night! What did he want?"

"Ten thousand dollars," replied Jasper.

"Ten thousand dollars!!" The lawyer's well-feigned surprise completed the deception practised upon Jasper. He did not, for an instant, suspect collusion between him and Martin.

"Yes; he very coolly proposed that I should lend him that sum, enable him to carry on some lead-mining operations in the west."

T. S. Arthur

"Preposterous!"

"So I told him."

"Well, what did he say?"

"Oh, he blustered, and made covert threats of exposure, of course."

"The scoundrel!" said Grind, fiercely.

"He's a villain double-dyed. I have never ceased to regret that we brought him into this business. We should have had a man of better spirit - of a nicer sense of honour."

"Yes, Mr. Jasper, that is true enough," replied Grind; "but the mischief is, your men of nicer honour are too squeamish for the kind of work in which we employed him. This is the defect in all such operations. Men cannot be thoroughly trusted."

The merchant sighed. He felt too deeply the force of Grind's remark.

"You know," said he, "this Martin better than I do. What is his character? Is he a mere blusterer, whose bark is worse than his bite; or is he vindictive and unscrupulous?"

"Both vindictive and unscrupulous. I must warn you not to provoke his ill-will. He would take delight in exposing all he knows about this business, if he is once fairly turned against you. A fast friend - he is a bitter enemy."

"But see what a price he demands for his friendship! I have already given him some five thousand dollars for his services, and now he demands ten more. In a year he will be back, and coolly seek to levy a contribution of twenty thousand dollars."

"I understood you to say that he only asked for a loan," remarks the lawyer.

"A loan! That's mere mockery. If you placed ten thousand dollars in his hands, would you ever expect to see the first copper of it again?"

Grind shrugged his shoulders.

"Of course you would not. It's a levy, not a loan - and so he, in his heart, regards it."

"He's a dangerous man," said the lawyer, "and it's to be regretted that you ever had any thing to do with him. But, now that your hand is in the lion's mouth, the wisest thing is to get it out with as little detriment as possible."

"Ten thousand dollars!" ejaculated the merchant. "Why, it's downright robbery! He might just as well stop me on the highway."

"It's a hard case, I must own, Mr. Jasper. You might resist him, and, at least not let him obtain what he demands without a struggle; but the question is, may you not receive a mortal wound in the contest."

"Ah! that is the rub, Grind. Rather than meet the exposure he could make, I would give twenty thousand dollars; yea, half, if not all I am worth."

Can wealth, held on such a tenure, and in such a state of mind, be called riches? Ah, no. How the possession is changed from a blessing into a curse!

"Then, Mr. Jasper," replied the lawyer, "there is but one course plain before you. If you make this man your enemy, he will surely pursue you to the death. There is no pity in him."

Jasper groaned aloud. Ere he could reply, the door of the office opened, and the individual about whom they were conversing entered. With the skill of practised actors, each instantly assumed a part, and hid, under a false exterior, their true states of mind. With something of cordiality each greeted the other: while side-glances, unobserved by Jasper, passed rapidly between Martin and the lawyer. A few commonplace inquiries and remarks followed, when Jasper made a movement to go, saying, as he did so -

"Mr. Martin, I will be pleased to see you some time to-day."

"Thank you; I will do myself the pleasure to call," was coolly answered. "At what time will you be most at leisure?"

"During the afternoon. Say at four or five o'clock."

"I will be there at four," returned Martin, in a bland voice, and with a courteous inclination of the head.

"Very well - you will find me in."

The merchant bowed to the accomplices - they were nothing better - and retired.

"Humph! I didn't expect to find him here quite so early," said Martin, with a sinister smile. "I rather guess I frightened him last night."

"I rather guess you did," returned the lawyer, his countenance reflecting the light that played on the other's face.

"Will the money come?" asked Martin.

"Undoubtedly."

"That's good. Ten thousand?"

"Yes."

"What did he say? He came to consult you, of course?"

"Yes."

"Well, what did he say?"

"More than I need take time to repeat. He is thoroughly frightened. That is enough for you to know."

"Ten thousand," said Martin musingly, and speaking to himself. "Ten thousand! That will do pretty well. But, if he will bleed for fifteen thousand, why may I not set the spring of my lancet a little deeper. I can make good use of my money."

"No - no," returned the lawyer quickly. "Ten thousand is enough. Don't play the dog and the shadow. This is over-greediness."

"Well - well. Just as you say. I can make him another friendly call in a year or so from this time."

The lawyer smiled in a way peculiar to himself, and then said -

"Hadn't you better be content with five thousand now. This goose will, no doubt, lay golden eggs for some years to come."

"A bird in the hand is worth two in the bush," was the quick answer. "I have gone in now for the ten thousand; and ten thousand I must have. I may be content with a smaller sum at my next appearance."

"You are to see him at four o'clock?" said Grind.

"Yes; that was the hour I named. So you must get all the necessary papers ready for me in time. I don't want to let him get the hitch on me of seeking to extort money. I only ask a loan, and will give bona-fide security on my lead-mine." Then, with one of his low chuckles, he added - "If he can get ten thousand dollars out of it, he will do more than any one else can. Ha! ha! ha!"

"The evidence of property, which you have," said Grind, "is all as it shows on the face?"

"It is, upon honour."

"Very well. Then I will draw the necessary papers, so that as little delay as possible need occur in the transference of security for the loan."

What further passed between the parties is of no consequence to the reader.

At four o'clock, precisely, Martin was at the store of Jasper.

"I hope to find you a little more reasonable today," said the merchant, with a forced smile, as the two men, after retiring to a remote part of the store, sat down and faced each other.

"I should be sorry to do any thing out of reason," returned Martin. His manner was more serious than Jasper's.

"I think your present demand out of reason," was answered.

"No good can possibly come, Mr. Jasper," said Martin, with a slight air of impatience, "out of an argument between you and I, on this subject. The sum I named to you last night I must have. Nothing less will meet my present want. But, understand me distinctly, I only ask it as a loan, and come prepared to give you the fullest security."

As Mr. Martin said this, he drew a package of papers from his pocket. "Here are the necessary documents," he added.

"Ten thousand dollars! Why, my dear sir, a sum like this is not to be picked up in the streets."

"I am very well aware of that," was the cool answer. "Had such been the case, I never would have troubled you with procuring the sum; nor would I have gone to the expense and fatigue of a long journey."

"You certainly ought to know enough of business, Martin, to

be aware that ten thousand dollars is not always to be commanded, even by the wealthiest, at a moment's notice."

"I do not ask the whole sum in cash," replied Martin. "Three or four thousand in ready money will do. Your notes at four and six months will answer very well for the balance."

But we will not record further what passed between these two men. It was all in vain that Jasper strove to escape; his adversary was too powerful. Ere they separated, Martin had in his possession, in cash and promissory notes, the sum of ten thousand dollars!

Already were the ill-gotten riches of Leonard Jasper taking to themselves wings. Unhappy man! How wretched was he during that and many succeeding days! Rolling, so to speak, in wealth, he yet possessed not life's highest blessing, a truly contented mind, flowing from conscious rectitude and an abiding trust in Providence. Without these, how poor is even he who counts his millions! With them, how rich is the humble toiler, who, receiving day by day his daily bread, looks up and is thankful!

CHAPTER XVII

A few weeks subsequent to the occurrences mentioned in the last chapter, Leonard Jasper received a call from Mr. Melleville, in whose service Claire still remained. The greeting of the two men was distant, yet courteous. A few words on current topics passed between them, after which Mr. Melleville said -

"I have called to ask you a question or two in regard to a child of the late Mr. Elder, to whom you are guardian."

The blood came instantly to the face of Jasper, who was not prepared for this; and in spite of his struggle to seem self-possessed, his eyes sank under those of his visitor. In a few moments, he recovered himself, and replied -

"The child, you mean, who is boarding with Edward Claire?"

"The same." The eyes of Melleville were fixed on those of Jasper so steadily, that the latter wavered, and, finally, again dropped to the floor.

"Well, I am ready to hear any thing that you have to say." Jasper had thrown off, once more, the vague sense of coming evil that made him cower under the steady gaze of Melleville.

"I learn," said the latter, "from Mr. Claire, that you refuse to pay any further sums for her maintenance. Is the property left by her father, to which common report has affixed considerable value, exhausted, or" -

"I have refused to pay *him* any further sums," said Jasper, in a quick, excited voice, interrupting Mr. Melleville. "Our contract, regularly entered into, has expired by limitation. He was to have the care of her only until she reached her twelfth year. Of this fact he is clearly advised, and I wonder at his pertinacity in endeavouring to retain the child, when he knows that I, her guardian, wish to have her in my own possession."

"He has had her ever since she was a little child; and both he and his wife are now strongly attached to her. In fact, she regards them as her parents; and their affection for her is not exceeded by their affection for their own children. To separate them would be exceedingly painful to all parties. As for the child, it would make her very unhappy."

"I can't help that, Mr. Melleville." Jasper spoke coldly.

"Under all the circumstances," said Mr. Melleville, after a pause, speaking slowly, and with considerable emphasis in his words, "it is my opinion that you had better let the child remain where she is."

"Why do you say so?" Jasper spoke with ill-concealed surprise; and the uneasy, suspicious manner, at first exhibited, returned.

"Claire regards the child as his own; and must so continue to regard her, even though taken out of his hands."

"Well, what of that?"

"It is for you, Mr. Jasper," was returned, "to determine for yourself, whether the surveillance of a man like Claire, who cannot now cease to feel a parent's interest in your ward, will be altogether agreeable."

"Surveillance! What do you mean? I don't understand this language. It looks like an effort to force me into measures. Pray, what have I to fear from Edward Claire?"

"Sometimes," replied Melleville, with a slow, meaning enunciation, "those we regard as most insignificant are the very ones we should most fear."

"Fear! Fear, Mr. Melleville! You make use of strange language."

"Perhaps I do," was answered. "And, as it seems unpleasant to you, I will say no more. I did not mean, when I called, to speak just as I have done. But, as the words have been uttered, I beg you to weigh them well, and to believe that they have a meaning. Good morning."

Jasper suppressed the utterance of the word "stay," which arose to his lips, and returned the bow of Mr. Melleville, who left without further remark.

"What can this mean?" Thus mused Leonard Jasper, when alone. "Can this scoundrel, Martin, have dropped a hint of the truth?" A slight shiver went through his nerves. "Something is wrong. There is suspicion in the thought of Melleville. I didn't look for trouble in this quarter."

To his own unpleasant reflections we will leave the merchant, and return to Edward Claire and his true-minded, loving-hearted wife.

For a week or two after the former entered upon his new duties as assistant clerk in a night-auction, he experienced no serious inconvenience from his more prolonged labours, although it did not escape the watchful eyes of his wife that his complexion was losing its freshness, and that his appetite was far from being so good as before. After this, he began to suffer oppressive weariness, that made the evening's toil a daily increasing burden. Then succeeded a feverish state, accompanied by pains in the head, back, and through the breast. Edith remonstrated, even with tears; but still Claire went nightly to his task, though each successive evening found him with less and less ability for its performance.

At last, he came home from the store of Mr. Melleville, at the usual tea-time, feeling so unwell that he was forced to lie down. He had no appetite for supper, and merely sipped part of a cup of tea brought to him by his wife as he still reclined upon the bed.

"Don't get up," said Edith, seeing her husband, after he had lain for some time, about to rise.

"I can't lie here any longer; it's nearly seven o'clock now."

"You're not going out to-night!"

"O yes; I must be at the store. There is no one to take my place, and the sales will begin by the time I can get there."

"But you are too sick to go out, Edward."

"I feel much better than I did, Edith. This little rest has refreshed me a great deal."

"No - no, Edward! You must not go away," said his wife in a distressed voice. "You are sick now, and the extra exertion of an evening may throw you into a serious illness."

"I feel a great deal better, dear," urged Claire. "But, sick or well, I must be there to-night, for the sale cannot go on without me. If I do not feel better to-morrow, I will ask Mr. F - to get some one, temporarily, in my place."

Still Edith opposed, but in vain.

By the time Claire arrived at the auction store, his head was throbbing with a pain so intense that he could scarcely see. Still, he resolutely persevered in his determination to go through, if possible, with the duties of the evening; and so, taking his place at his desk, as the auctioneer went upon the stand to cry the goods which had been advertised for sale, he prepared to keep the usual record of purchasers and prices.

This he was able to do for half an hour, when overtaxed and exhausted nature could bear up no longer.

"Mr. Claire," said the auctioneer, as he took in hand a new article, "did you make that last entry? - Mr. Jackson, ten cents a yard."

Claire's head had fallen over on the book in which he had been writing, and the auctioneer, supposing him only yielding to a momentary feeling of fatigue, or indolence, thus called his attention to his duties.

But Claire made no answer.

"Say! young man! Are you asleep!" The auctioneer spoke now with some sharpness of tone; but, as before, his words were not heeded.

"What's the matter, Mr. Claire? Are you sick?"

Still no response or movement.

"Mr. Claire! Bless me!" The auctioneer was now by his side, with his hand on him. "Bring some water, quick! He's fainted - or is dead! Here! some one help me to lay him down."

Two or three men came quickly behind the auctioneer's stand and assisted to lift the insensible man from the high stool on which he was seated, and place his body in a reclining position. Then water was dashed into his face, and various other means of restoration used. Full ten minutes passed before signs of returning life were exhibited. His recovery was very slow, and it was nearly an hour before he was well enough to be removed to his dwelling.

The shock of his appearance, supported from the carriage in which he had been conveyed home, by two men, was terrible to his wife, whose anxiety and fear had wrought her feelings already up to a high pitch of excitement.

"Oh! what is the matter? What has happened?" she cried, wringing her hands, while her face blanched to a deathly paleness.

"Don't be frightened," returned Claire, smiling feebly. "It was only a slight fainting fit. I'm over it now."

"That's all, madam," said the men who had brought him home. "He merely fainted. Don't be alarmed. It's all over."

After receiving the thanks of Claire and his assurances that he needed nothing further from their kindness, the men retired, and Edward then made every effort in his power to calm down the feelings of his wife, who continued weeping. This was no easy task, particularly as he was unable long to hide the many evidences of serious illness from which he was suffering. Against his remonstrance, so soon as she saw how it was with him, Mrs. Claire sent off the domestic for their family physician; who on learning the causes which led to the condition in which he found his patient, hesitated not to say that he must, as he valued his life, give up the night tasks he had imposed upon himself.

"Other men," said Claire, in answer to this, "devote quite as many hours to business."

"All men are not alike in constitution," returned the physician. "And even the strongest do not make overdrafts upon the system, without finding, sooner or later, a deficit in their health-account. As for you, nature has not given you the physical ability for great endurance. You cannot overtask yourself without a derangement of machinery."

How reluctantly, and with what a feeling of weakness, Claire acquiesced in this decision, the reader may imagine.

The morning found him something better, but not well enough to sit up. Mrs. Claire had, by this time, recovered in a measure her calmness and confidence. She had thought much, during the sleepless hours of the preceding night, and though the future was far from opening clearly to her straining vision, her mind rested in a well-assured confidence that all things would work together for their good. She knew in whom she trusted. On the Rock of Ages she had built the habitation where dwelt her higher hopes; and the storms of this world had no power to prevail against it.

How little dreamed gentle Fanny Elder - or Fanny Claire, as she was called - when she laid her cheek lovingly to that of her sick "father" - she knew him by no other name - and drew her arms around his neck, that he was suffering alone on her account. In her unselfish love, Claire felt a sweet compensation - while all he endured on her account had the effect to draw her, as it were, into his very heart.

As quickly as it could be done, Mrs. Claire got through with the most pressing of her morning duties, and then, the older children away to school, she came and sat down by her husband's bedside, and took his hand in hers. As he looked into her face, pale from sleeplessness and anxiety, tears filled his eyes.

"O, Edie!" said he, his voice tremulous with feeling, "isn't this disheartening? What *are* we to do?"

"*He* careth for us," was the low, calmly spoken reply; and, as Edith lifted a finger upward, a ray of heavenly confidence beamed in her countenance.

"I know, Edie; I know, but" -

The sick man left his sentence unfinished. A heavy sigh marking his state of doubt and darkness.

"We must feel as well as know, Edward," said his wife. "God is good. In looking back through all our past life, does not the retrospection lead to this undoubting conclusion? I am sure you will say yes. Has he not, in every case, proved better to us than all our fears? - Why, then, should we distrust him now? In the beautiful language of Cowper, let us say in these dark seasons -

> 'Judge not the Lord by feeble sense,
> But trust Him for His grace;
> Behind a frowning providence
> He hides a smiling face.
> His purposes will ripen fast,
> Unfolding every hour;
> The bud may have a bitter taste,
> But sweet will be the flower.'

"Shall we doubt the sun's existence, because the night has fallen? No, dear husband, no! There are bright stars smiling above us in token of his unerring return. We know that the morning cometh after a season of darkness; and so, after our spirits have lingered awhile in the realm of shadows, the light will break in from above. Has it not always been so, Edward?"

"He has led us by a way which we knew not."

The sick man's eyes were closed as he murmured these words; and his voice was slightly tremulous, yet expressive of a returning state of confidence.

"Yet, how safely," replied Edith. "When our feet were in slippery places, and we leaned on Him, did he not support us firmly? and when the mire and clay were deep in our path, did He not keep us from sinking therein?"

"He is goodness itself," said Claire, a calmer expression coming into his face. "It is wrong so to let doubt, distrust, and fear creep in and get possession of the heart; but, we are human - weakness and error are born with us. When the way in which we are walking is suddenly closed up before us, and we see the opening to no other way, how can we keep the faint heart from sinking?"

T. S. Arthur

"Only as Peter was saved from sinking. If we look to God, He will lift our hearts above the yielding billows. If we stand still, hopefully and trustingly, the high mountain before us will become as a plain, so that we can walk on in a smooth way, joyful and rejoicing."

"And so this high mountain, which has risen up so suddenly, will soon be cleft for us or levelled to a plain, if we wait patiently and confidingly for its removal?"

"Oh! I am sure of it, Edward," replied Mrs. Claire, with a beautiful enthusiasm. "We are His creatures, and He loves us with an infinite love. When his children are disposed to trust too much to the arm of flesh, He sometimes shows them their weakness in order that they may feel His strength. Faithfully and unselfishly, my husband, have you tried to meet the suddenly increased demand upon us: and this out of love for one of God's children. In the trial, weakness has prevailed over strength. Suddenly your hands have fallen to your side powerless. God saw it all; and permitted it all; and, in His own good time, will supply, from other sources, all that is really needed. We have the promise - our bread shall be given, and our water sure - not only the natural food that sustains outward life, but the true bread of heavenly affections, and the waters of pure truth, which nourish and sustain the spirit."

Edith ceased speaking. Her husband did not make an immediate reply; but lay pondering her words, and letting his thoughts expand their wings in the purer atmosphere into which she had lifted him.

After that they conversed together hopefully of the future; not that they saw the way more clearly before them, but heavenly confidence had taken the place of human distrust.

It was, perhaps, eleven o'clock in the day - the doctor had been there, and pronounced the condition of his patient favourable, but enjoined quiet and prolonged rest from either bodily or mental exertion - and the mind of Claire was beginning to run again in a slightly troubled channel.

"Here is a letter for you," said his wife, coming into the room, after a brief absence. "A young man just left it at the door."

Claire took the letter, wondering as he did so who it could be from. On breaking the seal, and unfolding it, he was greatly surprised to find within a check to his order for one hundred and fifty dollars, signed Leonard Jasper; and still more surprised to read the accompanying note, which was in these words:

"Enclosed you will find one hundred and fifty dollars, the sum due you for Fanny Elder's maintenance during the past and current quarter. When convenient, I should be glad to see you. Seeing that the child has remained with you so long, I don't know that it will be advisable to make a change now, although I had other views in regard to her. However, when you call, we can settle matters in regard to her definitively."

"Better to us than all our fears," murmured Claire, as he handed the letter to his wife, who read it with a truly thankful heart.

"Our way is smooth once more," she said, smiling through outpressing tears - "the mountain has become a level plain. All the dark clouds have been swept from our sky, and the sun is shining even more brightly than of old."

It was more than a week before Claire was sufficiently recovered to go out and attend to business as usual. At the first opportunity, he called upon Mr. Jasper, who received him with marked kindness of manner.

"I do not, now," said the merchant, "entertain the same views in regard to my ward that I did some time ago. Your opposition to my wishes then, fretted me a good deal; and I made up my mind, decisively, that so soon as she was twelve years of age, you must give her up. It was from this feeling that

T. S. Arthur

I acted when I refused to pay your last order. Since then, I have reflected a good deal on the subject; and reflection has modified, considerably, my feelings. I can understand how strong must be the attachment of both yourself and wife, and how painful the thought of separation from a long-cherished object of affection."

"The dread of separation, Mr. Jasper," replied Claire, "has haunted us during the last two years like an evil spirit."

"It need haunt you no more, Edward," was the kindly spoken reply. "If you still wish to retain the care of this child, you are free to do so."

"You have taken a mountain from my heart, Mr. Jasper," was the young man's feeling response.

"It is settled, then, Edward, that she remains with you. And now I must say a word about her education. I wish that to be thorough. She must have good advantages; better than the sum now paid for her maintenance will procure."

Claire made no reply, and Jasper continued -

"I have this to propose. The bulk of property left by her father is contained in two moderate-sized houses, one of which is at this time without a tenant. It is a very comfortable house for a small family. Just the thing, I should say, for you. If you will move into this house, you shall have it rent free, as a set-off to the increased charge Fanny will be to you in future. The three hundred per annum will be paid as usual. How will that do?"

"The compensation, I think, will be greater than the service," replied Claire.

"Not at all. During the next five or six years, or until she gains her majority, you will find the cost of clothing and education a constantly increasing sum. I know more about these things than you do. And I am very sure, since I understand your relation to her, that twice this expenditure, could not gain for her what she will have while in your care. As her guardian, I feel it my duty to provide liberally for her comfort and education, and to this you, of course, can have nothing to object."

And Claire did not object. In a few weeks from that time he removed into one of the houses mentioned by Jasper - a larger and far more comfortable one than that in which he had lived for several years. Here, with a thankful heart, he gathered his wife and children around him. How happy they all were! Not selfishly happy - if such contradictory terms may be used - but happy in the warmth of mutual love. A heaven on earth was this little household. Shall we contrast it with that of Leonard Jasper? No! - the opposite picture would leave upon the reader's mind too sad an impression; and we will not burden this chapter with another shadow.

CHAPTER XVIII

During the five or six following years, a number of events occurred bearing more or less seriously upon some of the actors in our story. With Edward Claire and his family, life had flowed on in an even current; and, but for the fact that his health never fairly recovered from the shock it received in consequence of his having taxed his physical system beyond its capability of endurance, the sunshine would never have been a moment from his threshold.

The important addition made to his income through the new arrangement volunteered by Fanny's guardian, gave to his external condition a more favourable aspect. He was no longer troubled about the ways and means of providing for his needful expenses. A much better situation, so far as a higher salary was concerned, had, during this time offered; but, as it required an amount of confinement and labour which he could not give, without endangering his health, he wisely declined the offer.

Far less smoothly had the current of Leonard Jasper's life flowed on. Twice during this period had he received visits from his old acquaintance, Martin, and each time he was made poorer by five thousand dollars. It was all in vain that he struggled and resisted. The man had no compassion in him. He cared not who suffered loss, so he was the gainer.

There were other miners at work sapping the foundations of Jasper's fortune, besides this less concealed operator. Parker, the young man who succeeded to the place of Claire, and who was afterward raised to the condition of partner, with a limited interest, was far from being satisfied with his dividend in the business. The great bulk of Jasper's means were used in outside speculations; and as the result of these became successively known to Parker, his thoughts began to run in a new channel. "If I only had money to go into this," and, "If I only had money to go into that," were words frequently on his tongue. He regarded himself as exceedingly shrewd; and confidently believed that, if he had capital to work with, he could soon amass an independent fortune.

"Money makes money," was his favourite motto.

Unscrupulous as his partner, it is not surprising that Parker, ere long, felt himself perfectly authorized to use the credit of the house in private schemes of profit. To do this safely, it was necessary to have a friend outside of the firm. Such a friend he did not find it very hard to obtain; and as nearly the whole burden of the business fell upon his shoulders, it was not at all difficult to hide every thing from Jasper.

Confident as Parker was in his great shrewdness, his speculations outside of the business did not turn out very favourably. His first essay was in the purchase of stocks, on which he lost, in a week, two thousand dollars.

Like the gamester who loses, he only played deeper, in the hope of recovering his losses; and as it often happens with the gamester, in similar circumstances, the deeper he played, the more he lost.

And so it went on. Sometimes the young man had a turn of good fortune, and sometimes all the chances went against him. But he was too far committed to recede without a discovery. There was no standing still; and so newer and bolder operations were tried, involving larger and larger sums of money, until the responsibilities of the firm, added to the large cash drafts made without the cognizance of Jasper, were enormous.

To all such mad schemes the end must come; and the end came in this instance. Failing to procure, by outside operations, sufficient money to meet several large notes, he was forced to divulge a part of his iniquity to Jasper, in order to save the credit of the firm. Suspicion of a deeper fraud being thereby aroused in the mind of his partner, time, and a sifting investigation of the affairs of the house, revealed the astounding fact that Parker had abstracted in money, and given the notes of the firm for his own use, to the enormous amount of fifty thousand dollars.

A dissolution of co-partnership took place in consequence. Parker, blasted in reputation, was dragged before a court of justice, in order to make him disgorge property alleged to be in his possession. But nothing could be found; and he was finally discharged from custody. The whole loss fell upon Jasper. He had nursed a serpent in his bosom, warming it with the warmth of his own life; and the serpent had stung him. Is it any wonder?

This circumstance, the discovery of Parker's fraudulent doings, took place about two years prior to the time when Fanny Elder attained her legal age.

The first thought of Jasper, after his separation from Parker, which took place immediately on discovering that he had used the credit of the firm improperly, was to send for Claire, and offer him a salary of a thousand dollars a year, to come in and fill the responsible position as clerk, from which Parker had just been ejected as partner.

"I can trust him fully," said Jasper to himself; "and I don't know anybody else that I can trust. He is honest; I will give him credit for that; too honest, it may be, for his own good. But, I don't know. Who would not rather be in his shoes than in Parker's?"

For some time Jasper's mind was favourable to making Claire the offer proposed, and he was about writing him a note, when a new view of the case struck him, dependent on the young man's relation to his ward, Fanny Elder.

"Oh no, no, no!" said he emphatically, speaking to himself - "that, I fear me, will not do. It would give him too open an access to my books, papers, and private accounts, in which are entries and memoranda that it might be dangerous for him to see."

Jasper sighed deeply as he finished this sentence, and then fell into a musing state. His thoughts, while this lasted, were not of the most self-satisfying character. Some serious doubts as to his having, in the main, pursued the wisest course in life, were injected into his mind; and, remarkable as it may seem for one so absorbed in the love of gain, there were moments when he almost envied the poor, but honest clerk, who had an approving conscience, and feared no man's scrutiny.

It was with no slight reluctance that he finally came to the conclusion that it would be altogether unsafe to take Claire into his employment. And so he cast about for some one to supply the place left vacant by Parker's withdrawal from the business. In his final selection he was not over-fortunate, as the result proved. The new clerk was shrewd, and capable enough, and apparently as much devoted to his employer's interests as Jasper could wish. Had not his own interests been regarded as paramount to those of the merchant, Jasper would have possessed in him a valuable assistant. But the clerk did not rise superior to temptations which came in his way. Jasper continued to trade on the close-cutting, overreaching, and unscrupulous system; and under such a teacher his clerk proved an apt learner.

"He cuts right and left," said he to himself, "and why may not I cut left and right when a good opportunity offers?"

Soon he began to "cut left and right," as he termed it, and it was not remarkable that, in his cutting operations, his employer occasionally suffered. The upshot was, after holding his situation a year, that several false entries, in his handwriting, were discovered in the books of Mr. Jasper. To what extent he robbed his employer, the latter never accurately knew; but he was worse off by at least three or four thousand dollars through his peculations.

Again the question of taking Claire once more into his employment came up in the mind of Jasper. After viewing it on every side, the decision was adverse. He felt that too great a risk was involved. And so he employed one in whom he could confide with less certainty.

Several years had now passed since the merchant began to feel the shock of adverse winds. All before was a summer sea, and the ship of his fortune had bent her sails alone to favouring breezes. But this was to be no longer. His ship had suffered not only by stress of weather, but also by the sacrifice of a portion of cargo to save what remained. And, at last, she was driving on toward the breakers, and her safety from destruction only hoped for through the activity, skill, and tireless vigilance of her helmsman.

A few years before, Mr. Jasper considered himself worth between two and three hundred thousand dollars; now, he passed sleepless nights in fear of impending ruin. He had trusted in riches; he had called them, in his heart, the greatest good. At his word they had poured in upon him from all sides, until he was half bewildered at sight of the glittering treasures; but, just as he began to feel secure in his possessions, they began to take themselves wings and fly away.

And, alas for him! he had laid up no other treasures. None in heaven; none in the hearts of his wife and children; none in his own mind. The staff upon which he had leaned was now a splintering reed, wounding as it bent under him.

CHAPTER XIX

There was one point of time to which Leonard Jasper looked with no little anxiety, and that was to the period of Fanny Elder's majority, when it was his purpose to relinquish his guardianship, and wash his hands, if it were possible to do so, entirely clean of her. Until the estate left by her father was settled up, the property in her hands and receipts in his, there was danger ahead. And, as the time drew nearer and nearer, he felt increasing uneasiness.

On the very day that Fanny reached her eighteenth year, Jasper sent a note to Claire, asking an interview.

"I wish," said he, when the latter came, "to have some conference with you about Miss Elder. She has now, you are no doubt aware, attained the legal age. Such being the case, I wish, as early as it can be done, to settle up the estate of her father, and pay over to her, or to any person she may select as her agent, the property in my hands. It has increased some in value. Will you consult her on the subject?"

Claire promised to do so; and, at the same time, asked as to the amount of Fanny's property.

"The total value will not fall much short of eight thousand dollars," replied Jasper. "There are two houses and lots that would sell at any time for six thousand dollars. You live in one of these houses, and the other is rented for two hundred and fifty dollars. Then there are nearly two thousand dollars in six per cent. stocks. When her father died, his estate consisted of these two houses, and a piece of poor land which he had taken as satisfaction for a debt. At the first opportunity, I sold the land and invested the money. This sum, with accumulations of interest, and rents received for several years, beyond what was required for Fanny's maintenance, has now increased to within a fraction of two thousand dollars, and is, as just said, invested in stocks. I think," added Jasper, "that you had better assume the management of this property yourself. Get from Miss Elder a power of attorney authorizing you to settle the estate, and the whole business can be completed in a very short time. I will make you out an accurate statement of every thing, so that you will be at no loss to comprehend the accounts."

To this there could, of course, be no objection on the part of Claire. He promised to confer with Fanny, and let Jasper know, in a day or two, the result.

Now came a new trial for Claire and his wife. They had taken Fanny, when only four years of age, and taken her so entirely into their home and affections, that she had almost from the first seemed to them as one of their own children. In a brief time the earlier memories of the child faded. The past was absorbed in the present; and she loved as parents none other than those she called by the tender names of "father" and "mother." The children with whom she grew up she knew only as her brothers and sisters. This thorough adoption and incorporation of the child into their family was not, in any sense, the work of design on the part of Claire and his wife. But they saw, in the beginning, no reason to check the natural tendency thereto. When little Fanny, of her own accord, addressed them, soon after her virtual adoption, as "father" and "mother," they accepted the child's own interpretation of their relative positions, and took her from that moment more entirely into their hearts.

And so Fanny Elder grew up to womanhood, in the full belief that she was the child of Mr. and Mrs. Claire. The new trial through which this excellent couple were now to pass, the reader can easily imagine. The time had come when Fanny must know the real truth in regard to herself - must be told that she had no natural claim upon the love of those whose love she prized above all things.

It seemed cruel to take away the conscious right to love and be loved, which had so long blessed her. And yet the truth must now be made known, and Mrs. Claire took upon herself the task of breaking it as gently as possible.

A woman in age and stature, yet with all the gentle deference of a daughter, Fanny moved by the side of Mrs. Claire with a loving thoughtfulness, daily sharing her household duties. Some months before she had left school, but was still taking lessons in music and French, and devoting a portion of time to practice in drawing, for which she had a decided taste.

On the day after Mr. Claire's interview with Jasper, Mrs. Claire said to Fanny, with a seriousness of tone and manner that brought a look of surprise to her face -

"Come to my room with me, dear. I have something to say to you."

Fanny moved along by her side, wondering to herself what could be in her mother's mind. On entering the chamber, Mrs. Claire shut the door, and then, as she sat down, with an arm around the young girl's waist, she said, in a thoughtful, earnest voice -

"Fanny, I want you to tell me the first thing you recollect in life."

"The first thing, mother?" She smiled at a request so unexpected, and Mrs. Claire smiled in return, though from a different cause.

"Yes, dear. I have a reason for asking this. Now, let your thoughts run back - far back, and recall for me the very first thing you can recollect."

The countenance of Fanny grew thoughtful, then serious, and then a half-frightened look flashed over it.

"Why, mother," said she, "what can you mean? What do you want to know?"

"Your first recollection, dear?" returned Mrs. Claire, with an assuring smile, although her heart was full, and it required the most active self-control to prevent her feelings from becoming manifest in her voice.

"Well, let me see! The first? The first? I was playing on the floor with a dear little baby? It was our Edie, wasn't it?"

"Yes - so far your memory is correct. I remember the time to which you refer as perfectly as if but a week had passed. Now, dear, try if you can recall any thing beyond that."

"Beyond that, mother? Oh, why do you ask? You make me feel so strangely. Can it be that some things I have thought to be only the memory of dreams, are indeed realities?"

"What are those things, my child?"

"I have a dim remembrance of a pale, but beautiful woman who often kissed and caressed me - of being in a sick-room - of a strange confusion in the house - of riding in a carriage with father to a funeral. Mother! is there any thing in this; if so, what does it mean?"

"That woman, Fanny," said Mrs. Claire, speaking with forced composure, "was your mother."

The face of the young girl grew instantly pale; her lips parted; and she gasped for breath. Then falling forward on the bosom of Mrs. Claire, she sobbed -

"Oh, mother! mother! How can you say this? It cannot, it cannot be. You are my own, my only mother."

"You did not receive your life through me, Fanny," replied Mrs. Claire, so soon as she could command her voice, for she too was overcome by feeling - "but in all else I am your mother, and I love you equally with my other children. If there has ever been a difference, it has all been in your favour."

"Why, why did you destroy the illusion under which I have so long rested?" said Fanny, when both were more composed. "Why tell me a truth from which no good can flow? Why break in upon my happy ignorance with such a chilling revelation? Oh, mother, mother! Forgive me, if I say you have been cruel."

"Not so, my child. Believe me, that nothing but duty would have ever driven me to this avowal. You are now at woman's legal age. You have a guardian, in whose hands your father, at his death, left, for your benefit, some property; and this person now desires to settle the estate, and transfer to you what remains."

Bewildered, like one awakening from a dream, Fanny listened to this strange announcement. And it was some time before she really comprehended her true position.

"Not your child - a guardian - property! - What does it all mean? Am I really awake, mother?"

"Yes, dear, you are awake. It is no dream, believe me," was the tender reply of Mrs. Claire. "But, remember, that all this does not diminish our love for you - does not remove you in the least from our affections. You are still our child, bound to us by a thousand intertwining chords."

But little more passed between them at this interview. Fanny asked for no more particulars, and Mrs. Claire did not think it necessary to give any further information. Fanny soon retired to her own chamber, there to commune with her thoughts, and to seek, in tears, relief to her oppressed feelings.

The meeting of Claire with Fanny, on his return home, was affecting. She met him with a quivering lip and moistened eyes, and, as she laid her cheek against his breast, murmured in a sad, yet deeply affectionate voice -

"My father!"

"My own dear child!" quickly replied Claire, with emotion.

And then both stood for some time silent. Leading her to a seat, Claire said tenderly -

"I have always loved you truly, and now you are dearer to me than ever."

"My more than father," was her simple response.

"My own dear child!" said Mr. Claire, kissing her fondly. "We have ever blessed the day on which you came to us from God."

Words would only have mocked their feelings, and so but few words passed between them, yet how full of thoughts crowding upon thoughts were their minds - how over-excited their hearts with new emotions of love.

After the younger members of the family had retired on that evening, Mr. and Mrs. Claire and Fanny were alone together. All three were in a calmer state of mind. Fanny listened with deep attention, her hand shading her countenance so as to conceal its varying expression, to a brief history of her parentage. Of things subsequent to the time of her entrance into her present home, but little was said. There was an instinctive delicacy on the part of Claire and his wife, now that Fanny was about coming into the possession of property, which kept back all allusion to the sacrifices they had made, and the pain they had suffered on her account, in their contentions with her guardian. In fact, this matter of property produced with them a feeling of embarrassment. They had no mercenary thoughts in regard to it - had no wish to profit by their intimate and peculiar relation. And yet, restricted in their own income, and with a family growing daily more expensive, they understood but too well the embarrassment which would follow, if any very important change were made in their present external relations. To explain every thing to Fanny, would, they knew, lead to an instant tender of all she possessed. But this they could not do; nor had they a single selfish desire in regard to her property. If things could remain as they were, without injustice to Fanny, they would be contented; but they were not altogether satisfied as to the amount they were receiving for her maintenance. It struck them as being too much; and they had more than once conferred together in regard to its reduction.

The first thing to be done was to make Fanny comprehend her relation to Mr. Jasper, her guardian, and his wish to settle up the estate of her father, and transfer to her, or her representative, the property that remained in his hands.

"I will leave all with you, father," was the very natural response made to this. "All I have is yours. Do just as you think best."

On the next day a power of attorney in the name of Edward Claire was executed; and, as Jasper was anxious to get the business settled, every facility thereto was offered. Claire examined the will of Mr. Elder, in which certain property was mentioned, and saw that it agreed with the guardian's statement. All the accounts were scrutinized; and all the vouchers for expenditure compared with the various entries. Every thing appeared correct, and Claire expressed himself entirely satisfied. All legal forms were then complied with; and, in due time, the necessary documents were prepared ready for the signature of Claire, by which Jasper would be freed from the nervous anxiety he had for years felt whenever his thoughts went forward to this particular point of time.

On the evening preceding the day when a consummation so long and earnestly looked for was to take place, Jasper, with his mind too much absorbed in business troubles to mingle with his family, sat alone in his library, deeply absorbed in plans and calculations. His confidence in fortune and his own prudence had been growing weaker, daily; and now it seemed to him as if a great darkness were gathering all around. He had fully trusted in himself; alas! how weak now seemed to him his human arm; how dim the vision with which he would penetrate the future. He was mocked of his own overweening and proud confidence.

This was his state of mind when a servant came to the library-door, and announced a gentleman who wished to see him.

"What is his name?" asked Jasper.

"He said it was no difference. He was a friend."

"It might make a great difference," Jasper muttered in an undertone. "Show him up," he said aloud.

The servant retired, and Jasper waited for his visitor to appear. He was not long in suspense. The door soon reopened, and a man, poorly clad, and with a face bearing strong marks of intemperance and evil passions, came in.

"You do not know me," said he, observing that the merchant, who had risen to his feet, did not recognise him.

Jasper shook his head.

"Look closer." There was an air of familiarity and rude insolence about the man.

"Martin!" exclaimed Jasper, stepping back a few paces. "Is it possible!"

"Quite possible, friend Jasper," returned the man, helping

himself to a chair, and sinking into it with the air of one who felt himself at home.

Surprise and perplexity kept the merchant dumb for some moments. He would quite as lief have been confronted with a robber, pistol in hand.

"I do not wish to see you, Martin," said he, at length, speaking in a severe tone of voice. "Why have you intruded on me again? Are you not satisfied? Have you no mercy?"

"None, Leonard Jasper, none," replied the man scowling. "I never knew the meaning of the word - no more than yourself."

"You are nothing better than a robber," said the merchant, bitterly.

"I only share with bolder robbers their richer plunder," retorted the man.

"I will not bear this, Martin. Leave my presence."

"I will relieve you certainly," said the visitor, rising, "when you have done for me what I wish. I arrived here, to-day, penniless; and have called for a trifling loan to help me on my way North."

"Loan! what mockery! I will yield no further to your outrageous demands. I was a fool ever to have feared the little power you possess. Go, sir! I do not fear you."

"I want your check for two hundred dollars - no more," said Martin, in a modified tone - "I will not be hard on you. Necessity drives me to this resort; but I hope never to trouble you again."

"Not a dollar," replied Jasper, firmly. "And now, my friend, seek some other mode of sustaining yourself in vice and idleness. You have received from me your last contribution. In

T. S. Arthur

settling the estate of Reuben Elder to the entire satisfaction of all parties, I have disarmed you. You have no further power to hurt."

"You may find yourself mistaken in regard to my power," replied Martin as he made a movement toward the door, and threw back upon the merchant a side-glance of the keenest malignity. "Many a foot has been stung by the reptile it spurned."

The word "stay" came not to Jasper's lips. He was fully in earnest. Martin paused, with his hand on the door, and said -

"One hundred dollars will do."

"Not a copper, if it were to save you from the nether regions!" cried Jasper, his anger and indignation o'erleaping the boundaries of self-control.

He was alone in the next moment. As his excitement cooled down, he felt by no means indifferent to the consequences which might follow this rupture with Martin. More than one thought presented itself, which, if it could have been weighed calmly a few minutes before, would have caused a slightly modified treatment of his unwelcome visitor.

But having taken his position, Jasper determined to adhere to it, and brave all consequences.

While Claire was yet seated at the breakfast-table on the next morning, word was brought that a gentleman was in the parlour and wished to see him.

On entering the parlour, he found there a man of exceedingly ill appearance, both as to countenance and apparel.

"My name is Martin," said this person - "though you do not, I presume, know me."

Claire answered that he was to him an entire stranger.

"I have," said the man, speaking in a low, confidential tone of voice, "became cognisant of certain facts, which it much concerns you, or at least your adopted daughter, Fanny Elder, to know."

For a few moments, Claire was overcome with surprise.

"Concerns Fanny Elder to know! What do you mean, sir?"

"Precisely what I say. There has been a great fraud committed; and I know all the ins and the outs of it!"

"By whom?" asked Claire.

"Ah!" replied the visitor, "that we will come to after a while."

"Upon whom, then?"

"Upon the estate of Ruben Elder, the father of your adopted daughter."

Not liking either the man's appearance or manner, Claire said, after a moment's reflection -

"Why have you called to see me?"

"To give the information I have indicated - provided, of course, that you desire to have it."

"On what terms do you propose to act in this matter? Let us understand each other in the beginning."

"I can put you in the way of recovering for Miss Elder from twenty to a hundred thousand dollars, out of which she has been cheated. But, before I give you any information on the subject, I shall require an honourable pledge on your part, as well as written agreement, to pay me twenty per cent. of the

T. S. Arthur

whole amount recovered. Will you give it?"

Claire bent his head in thought for some moments. When he looked up he said -

"No, sir. I can make no compact with you of this kind."

"Very well, sir. That closes the matter," replied Martin, rising. "If you will not buy a fortune at so small a cost, you deserve to be poor. How far your conscience is clear in respect to Miss Elder, is another matter. But, perhaps you don't credit what I say. Let me give you a single hint. Fanny Elder was missing once for three days. I had a hand in that affair. Do you think she was carried off, and taken to another city for nothing? If so, you are wonderfully mistaken. But good morning, sir. If you should, on reflection, change your mind, you can hear of me by calling at the office of Grind, the lawyer."

"Good morning," returned Claire, showing not the least disposition to retain the man, toward whom he experienced a strong feeling of dislike and sense of repulsion.

Martin lingered a few moments, and then went out, leaving Claire bewildered by a rush of new thoughts.

CHAPTER XX

The meeting of Claire and Jasper, for the final settlement of Mr. Elder's estate, was to take place at the office of Grind, at ten o'clock. Before keeping his appointment, the former turned over in his mind, with careful deliberation, the circumstances which had just occurred; and the more he thought of it, the better satisfied was he that a fraud had been committed. The author of that fraud could be no one else but the guardian of Fanny; of whose honesty Claire had, with good reason, no very high opinion. His conclusion was, not to accept, at present, a settlement of the estate.

With an uneasy foreboding of evil - he was, in fact, rarely now without that feeling - Leonard Jasper took his way to the office of Grind. Notwithstanding he had defied Martin, he yet feared him. But he was so near to the point of comparative safety, that he hoped soon to be past all real danger from this quarter. Too little time had elapsed, since he parted with him, for Martin to see Claire, even if a thought of assailing him in that quarter had crossed his mind. So Jasper believed. How sadly taken by surprise was he, therefore, when, on meeting Claire, the latter said -

"Since I saw you yesterday, a matter has come to my knowledge which I feel bound to investigate, before procee-ding any farther in this business."

As if struck by a heavy blow, Jasper moved a pace or two backward, while an instant pallor overspread his face. Quickly

T. S. Arthur

recovering himself, he said -

"Explain yourself, Edward. What matter has come to your knowledge?"

"On that subject I would prefer speaking with you alone," replied Claire.

"This room is at your service," said Grind, rising and retiring toward his front office. "You will be altogether free from intrusion." And he passed out, closing the door behind him.

"Edward," said Jasper, in as firm a voice as he could assume, "What is the meaning of this? You look at me with an expression of countenance, and have spoken in a tone that implies a belief on your part that I have not acted fairly in the matter of this guardianship."

"Such, at least, is my impression," replied Claire, firmly.

"Have you come here to insult me, sir?" Jasper drew himself up with an offended manner.

"No, Mr. Jasper. I have no such intention. All I purpose is, to ascertain how far certain information received by me this morning is correct."

"What information?"

The merchant became a good deal agitated.

"A man named Martin called on me" -

"Martin! oh, the wretch! My curses rest on him, for a base betrayer!"

Claire was startled at the effect produced by his mention of the name of Martin. Jasper, on hearing this name, believed that every thing had been divulged, and, in the bitterness and despair of this conviction, threw off all concealment. His countenance, which had partly gained its usual colour, became pallid again, while large beads of sweat oozed from the relaxed pores and stood upon his forehead. Moving back a step or two, he sank into a chair, and averting his face, sat struggling with himself to regain the mastery over his feelings.

How changed, in a few brief years, had become the relation of these two men. The poor, humble, despised, but honest clerk, now stood erect, while the merchant cowered before him in humiliation and fear.

"Edward," said Jasper, as soon as he had sufficient composure of mind to think somewhat clearly and speak calmly, "What do you purpose doing in this matter?"

"What is right, Mr. Jasper," answered Claire, firmly. "That is my duty."

"Ruin! ruin! ruin!" exclaimed Jasper, in a low voice, again losing command of himself, and wringing his hands hopelessly. "Oh! that it should have come to this!"

Astonished as Claire was by what he now heard and saw, he felt the necessity of preserving the most entire self-possession. When Jasper again put the question -

"What do you purpose doing, Edward?" he replied.

"I shall be better able to answer that question when I have all the particulars upon which to make up a decision. At present, I only know that a large amount of property has been withheld from Miss Elder; and that I have only to bring this man Martin into a court of justice to have every thing made clear."

"And this you purpose doing?"

"I shall do so, undoubtedly; unless the object to be gained by such a course is secured in another way."

T. S. Arthur

"Quite as much, believe me, Edward, can be gained through private arrangement as by legal investigation," returned Jasper, his manner greatly subdued. "You and I can settle every thing, I am sure, between ourselves; and, as far as my ability will carry me, it shall be to your entire satisfaction. I have greatly mistaken your character, or you will take no pleasure in destroying me."

"Pleasure in destroying you?" Claire was still further affected with surprise. "In no man's destruction could I take pleasure."

"I believe you Edward. And now let me give you a history of this matter from the beginning. You will know better what course to pursue when you comprehend it fully."

And then, to the astonished ears of Claire, Jasper related how, through the man Martin, he became possessed of the fact that the supposed almost valueless piece of land in Pennsylvania which Mr. Elder had taken to secure a debt of five hundred dollars, contained a rich coal deposite - and how, as executor to his estate, and the guardian of his child, he had by presenting the child in person before commissioners appointed by the court, obtained an order for the sale of the land, with the declared purpose of investing the proceeds in some productive property. It was for this that he had been so anxious to get Fanny, and for this that he carried her off forcibly, although his agency in the matter did not appear. He then related how, in the sale, he became the real purchaser; and how, afterward, the tract, as coal land, was sold to a company for nearly a hundred thousand dollars.

"But Edward," said Jasper, as he concluded his humiliating narrative, "I am worse off to-day than if I had never made this transaction. It gave me a large amount of capital for trade and speculation, but it also involved me in connections, and led me into schemes for money-making, that have wellnigh proved my ruin. In all truth, I am not, this day, worth one-half of what I received for that property."

Jasper ceased speaking; but astonishment kept Claire silent.

"And now, Edward," resumed the former, "I am ready to make restitution as far as in my power lies. You can drag me into court, and thus blast my reputation; or, you can obtain for Miss Elder as much, or even more, than you would probably get by law - for, if driven into the courts, I will contend to the last moment - through an amicable arrangement. Which course are you disposed to take?"

"I have no desire to harm you, Mr. Jasper - none in the world. If the terms of settlement which you may offer are such as, under all the circumstances, I feel justified in accepting, I will meet your wishes. But you must bear in mind that, in this matter, I am not acting for myself."

"I know - but your judgment of the case must determine."

"True - and in that judgment I will endeavour to hold an equal balance."

The two men now retired from the lawyer's office; and, ere parting, arranged a meeting for that evening at the store of Jasper, where they could be entirely alone. For two or three successive evenings these conferences were continued, until Claire was entirely satisfied that the merchant's final offer to transfer to the possession of Fanny Elder four houses, valued at five thousand dollars each, in full settlement of her father's estate, was the very best he could do; and far more than he would probably obtain if an appeal were made to the law.

As quickly as this transfer could be made, it was done. Not until the long-desired documents, vouching for the equitable settlement of the estate, were in Jasper's hands, did he breathe freely. Oh! through what an ordeal he had passed. How his own pride, self-consequence, and self-sufficiency had been crushed out of him! And not only in spirit was he humbled and broken. In his anxiety to settle up the estate of Mr. Elder, and thus get the sword that seemed suspended over his head by a single hair, removed, he had overstepped his ability. The houses referred to were burdened with a mortgage of nearly ten thousand dollars; this had, of course, to be released; and, in procuring the money therefor, he strained to the utmost his credit, thus cutting off important facilities needed in his large, and now seriously embarrassed business.

It is the last pound that breaks the camel's back. This abstraction of money and property took away from Jasper just what he needed to carry him safely through a period of heavy payments, at a time when there was some derangement in financial circles. In less than a month from the time he settled the estate of Reuben Elder, the news of his failure startled the business community. He went down with a heavy plunge, and never again rose to the surface. His ruin was complete. He had trusted in riches. Gold was his god; and the idol had mocked him.

CHAPTER XXI

Beyond what has already been written, there is not much, in the histories of those whom we have introduced, to be told, except briefly, worthy the reader's interested attention.

Martin, the old accomplice of Jasper, finding his power over that individual gone, and failing in the card he played against Claire's nice sense of honour and integrity of purpose, now turned, like an ill-natured, hungry cur, and showed his teeth to the man through whose advice he had so long been able to extort money from Jasper. He felt the less compunction in so doing, from the fact that Grind, angry with him for having been the agent of Jasper's final destruction, which involved him in a severe loss, had expressed himself in no measured terms - had, in fact, lashed him with most bitter and opprobrious words.

Several times, during the progress of events briefly stated in the concluding portions of the last chapter, Martin had, in his frequent visits to the lawyer, hinted, more or less remotely, at his great need of money. But to these intimations, Grind never gave the slightest response. At last the man said boldly -

"Mr. Grind, you must help me to a little money." This was directly after the failure of Jasper.

"I cannot do it," was the unequivocal reply. "You have, by your miserable vindictiveness, ruined Jasper, after having subsisted on him for years - base return for all you owe him -

and, in doing so, half destroyed me. You have killed the goose that laid the golden egg, and there is no one but yourself to thank for this folly."

"You must help me, Mr. Grind," said Martin, his brows knitting, and the muscles of his lips growing rigid. "You had a hand in that business as well as Jasper; you took a big slice, if he did keep the major part of the loaf; and so I have a right to ask some slight return for important service rendered."

"What! This to me!" exclaimed Grind, roused to instant excitement.

"This to you," was the cool, deliberate answer.

"You have mistaken your man," returned the lawyer, now beginning to comprehend Martin more thoroughly. "I understand my whole relation to this affair too well to be moved by any attempt at extortion which you can make. But I can tell you a little secret, which it may be interesting for you to know."

"What is it?" growled the man.

"Why, that I hold the power to give you a term in the State's prison, whenever I may happen to feel inclined that way."

"Indeed!" Martin spoke with a cold, defiant sneer.

"I am uttering no vague threat. From the beginning, I have kept this trap over you, ready to spring, if need be, at a moment's warning."

"I suppose you thought me a poor fool, did you not?" said Martin as coldly and contemptuously as before. "But you were mistaken. I have not been altogether willing to trust myself in your hands, without good advice from a limb of the law quite as shrewd as yourself."

"What do you mean?" exclaimed Grind, somewhat startled by so unexpected a declaration.

"Plainly," was answered, "while I took your advice as to the surest way to act upon Jasper, I consulted another as to the means of protecting myself from you, if matters ever came to a pinch."

"Oh! Preposterous!" Grind forced a laugh. "That's only an afterthought."

"Is it. Hark!" Martin bent close to his ear, and uttered a few words in an undertone. Grind started as if stung by a serpent.

"Wretch!"

"It is useless to call ill names, my friend. I have you in my power; and I mean to keep you there. But I shall not be very hard on you. So, don't look so awfully cut down."

For once the scheming, unscrupulous lawyer found himself outwitted. His tool had proved too sharp for him. Without a doubt he was in his power to an extent by no means agreeable to contemplate. Grind now saw that conciliation was far better than antagonism.

When Martin retired from the lawyer's office, he had in his pocket a check for two hundred dollars, while behind him was left his solemn pledge to leave the city for New Orleans the next day. The pledge, when given, he did not intend to keep; and it was not kept, as Grind soon afterward learned, to his sorrow. A drunkard and a gambler, it did not take Martin long to see once more the bottom of his purse. Not until this occurred did he trouble the lawyer again. Then he startled him with a second visit, and, after a few sharp words, came off with another check, though for a less amount.

And for years, leech-like, Martin, sinking lower and lower all the time, continued his adhesion to the lawyer, abstracting

T. S. Arthur

continually, but in gradually diminishing sums, the money needed for natural life and sensual indulgence, until often his demands went not above a dollar. Grind, reluctantly as he yielded to these demands, believed it wiser to pay them than to meet the exposure Martin had it in his power to make. And so it went on, until, one day, to his inexpressible relief, Grind read in the morning papers an account of the sudden and violent death of his enemy. His sleep was sounder on the night that followed than it had been for a long, long time.

Of Edward Claire, and his happy family - not happy merely from an improved external condition, for the foundation of their happiness was laid in a deeper ground - we have not much to relate.

When Claire brought to Fanny the title-deeds of the property which he had recovered from Jasper, she pushed them back upon him, saying, as she did so -

"Keep them, father - keep them. All is yours."

"No, my dear child," replied Claire, seriously, yet with tenderness and emotion, "all is not mine. All is yours. This property, through a wise Providence, has come into your possession. I have no right to it."

"If it is mine, father," said Fanny, "have I not a right to do with it what I please?"

"In a certain sense you have."

"Then I give it all to you - you, my more than father!"

"For such a noble tender, my dear child, I thank you in the very inmost of my heart. But I cannot accept of it, Fanny."

"Why not, father? Why not? You have bestowed on me more than wealth could buy! I know something of what you have borne and suffered for me. Your health, now impaired, was broken for me. Oh, my father! Can I ever forget that? Can I ever repay you all I owe? Were the world's wealth mine, it should be yours."

Overcome by her feelings, Fanny wept for some time on the breast of him she knew only as her father; and there the interview closed for the time.

Soon after it was renewed; and the occasion of this was an advantageous business offer made to Claire by Mr. Melleville, if he could bring in a capital of twelve thousand dollars. Two of the houses received from Jasper, with some stocks, were sold to furnish this capital, and Claire, after his long struggle, found himself in a safe and moderately profitable business; and, what was more, with a contented and thankful spirit. Of what treasures was he possessed? Treasures of affection, such as no money could buy; and, above all, the wealth of an approving conscience.

Mrs. Claire - happy wife and mother! - how large too was her wealth. From the beginning she had possessed the riches which have no wings - spiritual riches, that depend on no worldly changes; laid up in the heaven of her pure mind, where moth could not corrupt, nor thieves break through and steal. The better worldly fortune that now came added to her happiness, because it afforded the means of giving to their children higher advantages, and procured for them many blessings and comforts to which they were hitherto strangers.

Five years, passed under an almost cloudless sky, succeeded, and then the sweet home circle was broken by the withdrawal of one whose presence made perpetual sunshine. One so good, so lovely, so fitted in every way to form the centre of another home circle as Fanny Elder, could hardly remain unwooed or unwon. Happily, in leaving the paternal haven, her life-boat was launched on no uncertain sea. The character of her husband was based on those sound, religious principles, which regard justice to man as the expression of love to God.

T. S. Arthur

A few weeks after the husband of Fanny had taken his lovely young wife to his own home, Claire waited upon him for the purpose of making a formal transfer of his wife's property.

"There are four houses," said Claire, in describing the property; "besides twelve thousand dollars which I have in my business. A portion of this latter I will pay over; on the balance, while it remains" -

"Mr. Claire," returned the young man, interrupting him, "the house you now live in, Fanny says, is your property - also the capital in your business."

"No - no - no. This is not so. I do not want, and I will not keep a dollar of her patrimony."

"You are entitled to every thing, in good right," said the young man, smiling. "But we will consent to take one-half as a good start in life."

"But, my dear sir" -

We will not, however, record the arguments, affirmations, protestations, etc., made by each party in this contention, but drop the curtain, and leave the reader to infer the sequel. He cannot go very far wide of the truth.

Choose from Thousands of 1stWorldLibrary Classics By

A. M. Barnard
Ada Leverson
Adolphus William Ward
Aesop
Agatha Christie
Alexander Aaronsohn
Alexander Kielland
Alexandre Dumas
Alfred Gatty
Alfred Ollivant
Alice Duer Miller
Alice Turner Curtis
Alice Dunbar
Allen Chapman
Ambrose Bierce
Amelia E. Barr
Amory H. Bradford
Andrew Lang
Andrew McFarland Davis
Andy Adams
Anna Alice Chapin
Anna Sewell
Annie Besant
Annie Hamilton Donnell
Annie Payson Call
Annie Roe Carr
Annonaymous
Anton Chekhov
Arnold Bennett
Arthur Conan Doyle
Arthur M. Winfield
Arthur Ransome
Arthur Schnitzler
Atticus
B.H. Baden-Powell
B. M. Bower
B. C. Chatterjee
Baroness Emmuska Orczy
Baroness Orczy
Basil King
Bayard Taylor
Ben Macomber
Bertha Muzzy Bower
Bjornstjerne Bjornson
Booth Tarkington
Boyd Cable
Bram Stoker
C. Collodi
C. E. Orr

C. M. Ingleby
Carolyn Wells
Catherine Parr Traill
Charles A. Eastman
Charles Amory Beach
Charles Dickens
Charles Dudley Warner
Charles Farrar Browne
Charles Ives
Charles Kingsley
Charles Klein
Charles Hanson Towne
Charles Lathrop Pack
Charles Romyn Dake
Charles Whibley
Charles Willing Beale
Charlotte M. Braeme
Charlotte M. Yonge
Charlotte Perkins Stetson
Clair W. Hayes
Clarence Day Jr.
Clarence E. Mulford
Clemence Housman
Confucius
Coningsby Dawson
Cornelis DeWitt Wilcox
Cyril Burleigh
D. H. Lawrence
Daniel Defoe
David Garnett
Dinah Craik
Don Carlos Janes
Donald Keyhoe
Dorothy Kilner
Dougan Clark
Douglas Fairbanks
E. Nesbit
E.P.Roe
E. Phillips Oppenheim
Earl Barnes
Edgar Rice Burroughs
Edith Van Dyne
Edith Wharton
Edward Everett Hale
Edward J. O'Biren
Edward S. Ellis
Edwin L. Arnold
Eleanor Atkins
Eliot Gregory

Elizabeth Gaskell
Elizabeth McCracken
Elizabeth Von Arnim
Ellem Key
Emerson Hough
Emilie F. Carlen
Emily Dickinson
Enid Bagnold
Enilor Macartney Lane
Erasmus W. Jones
Ernie Howard Pie
Ethel May Dell
Ethel Turner
Ethel Watts Mumford
Eugenie Foa
Eugene Wood
Eustace Hale Ball
Evelyn Everett-green
Everard Cotes
F. H. Cheley
F. J. Cross
F. Marion Crawford
Federick Austin Ogg
Ferdinand Ossendowski
Francis Bacon
Francis Darwin
Frances Hodgson Burnett
Frances Parkinson Keyes
Frank Gee Patchin
Frank Harris
Frank Jewett Mather
Frank L. Packard
Frank V. Webster
Frederic Stewart Isham
Frederick Trevor Hill
Frederick Winslow Taylor
Friedrich Kerst
Friedrich Nietzsche
Fyodor Dostoyevsky
G.A. Henty
G.K. Chesterton
Gabrielle E. Jackson
Garrett P. Serviss
Gaston Leroux
George A. Warren
George Ade
Geroge Bernard Shaw
George Durston
George Ebers

George Eliot
George Gissing
George MacDonald
George Meredith
George Orwell
George Sylvester Viereck
George Tucker
George W. Cable
George Wharton James
Gertrude Atherton
Gordon Casserly
Grace E. King
Grace Gallatin
Grace Greenwood
Grant Allen
Guillermo A. Sherwell
Gulielma Zollinger
Gustav Flaubert
H. A. Cody
H. B. Irving
H.C. Bailey
H. G. Wells
H. H. Munro
H. Irving Hancock
H. Rider Haggard
H. W. C. Davis
Haldeman Julius
Hall Caine
Hamilton Wright Mabie
Hans Christian Andersen
Harold Avery
Harold McGrath
Harriet Beecher Stowe
Harry Castlemon
Harry Coghill
Harry Houidini
Hayden Carruth
Helent Hunt Jackson
Helen Nicolay
Hendrik Conscience
Hendy David Thoreau
Henri Barbusse
Henrik Ibsen
Henry Adams
Henry Ford
Henry Frost
Henry James
Henry Jones Ford
Henry Seton Merriman
Henry W Longfellow
Herbert A. Giles

Herbert Carter
Herbert N. Casson
Herman Hesse
Hildegard G. Frey
Homer
Honore De Balzac
Horace B. Day
Horace Walpole
Horatio Alger Jr.
Howard Pyle
Howard R. Garis
Hugh Lofting
Hugh Walpole
Humphry Ward
Ian Maclaren
Inez Haynes Gillmore
Irving Bacheller
Isabel Hornibrook
Israel Abrahams
Ivan Turgenev
J.G.Austin
J. Henri Fabre
J. M. Barrie
J. Macdonald Oxley
J. S. Fletcher
J. S. Knowles
J. Storer Clouston
Jack London
Jacob Abbott
James Allen
James Andrews
James Baldwin
James Branch Cabell
James DeMille
James Joyce
James Lane Allen
James Lane Allen
James Oliver Curwood
James Oppenheim
James Otis
James R. Driscoll
Jane Austen
Jane L. Stewart
Janet Aldridge
Jens Peter Jacobsen
Jerome K. Jerome
John Burroughs
John Cournos
John F. Kennedy
John Gay
John Glasworthy

John Habberton
John Joy Bell
John Kendrick Bangs
John Milton
John Philip Sousa
Jonas Lauritz Idemil Lie
Jonathan Swift
Joseph A. Altsheler
Joseph Carey
Joseph Conrad
Joseph E. Badger Jr
Joseph Hergesheimer
Joseph Jacobs
Jules Vernes
Julian Hawthrone
Julie A Lippmann
Justin Huntly McCarthy
Kakuzo Okakura
Kenneth Grahame
Kenneth McGaffey
Kate Langley Bosher
Kate Langley Bosher
Katherine Cecil Thurston
Katherine Stokes
L. A. Abbot
L. T. Meade
L. Frank Baum
Latta Griswold
Laura Dent Crane
Laura Lee Hope
Laurence Housman
Lawrence Beasley
Leo Tolstoy
Leonid Andreyev
Lewis Carroll
Lewis Sperry Chafer
Lilian Bell
Lloyd Osbourne
Louis Hughes
Louis Tracy
Louisa May Alcott
Lucy Fitch Perkins
Lucy Maud Montgomery
Luther Benson
Lydia Miller Middleton
Lyndon Orr
M. Corvus
M. H. Adams
Margaret E. Sangster
Margret Howth
Margaret Vandercook

Margret Penrose
Maria Edgeworth
Maria Thompson Daviess
Mariano Azuela
Marion Polk Angellotti
Mark Overton
Mark Twain
Mary Austin
Mary Catherine Crowley
Mary Cole
Mary Hastings Bradley
Mary Roberts Rinehart
Mary Rowlandson
M. Wollstonecraft Shelley
Maud Lindsay
Max Beerbohm
Myra Kelly
Nathaniel Hawthrone
Nicolo Machiavelli
O. F. Walton
Oscar Wilde
Owen Johnson
P.G. Wodehouse
Paul and Mabel Thorne
Paul G. Tomlinson
Paul Severing
Percy Brebner
Peter B. Kyne
Plato
R. Derby Holmes
R. L. Stevenson
R. S. Ball
Rabindranath Tagore
Rahul Alvares
Ralph Bonehill
Ralph Henry Barbour
Ralph Victor
Ralph Waldo Emmerson
Rene Descartes
Rex Beach

Rex E. Beach
Richard Harding Davis
Richard Jefferies
Richard Le Gallienne
Robert Barr
Robert Frost
Robert Gordon Anderson
Robert L. Drake
Robert Lansing
Robert Lynd
Robert Michael Ballantyne
Robert W. Chambers
Rosa Nouchette Carey
Rudyard Kipling
Samuel B. Allison
Samuel Hopkins Adams
Sarah Bernhardt
Sarah C. Hallowell
Selma Lagerlof
Sherwood Anderson
Sigmund Freud
Standish O'Grady
Stanley Weyman
Stella Benson
Stella M. Francis
Stephen Crane
Stewart Edward White
Stijn Streuvels
Swami Abhedananda
Swami Parmananda
T. S. Ackland
T. S. Arthur
The Princess Der Ling
Thomas A. Janvier
Thomas A Kempis
Thomas Anderton
Thomas Bailey Aldrich
Thomas Bulfinch
Thomas De Quincey
Thomas Dixon

Thomas H. Huxley
Thomas Hardy
Thomas More
Thornton W. Burgess
U. S. Grant
Valentine Williams
Various Authors
Vaughan Kester
Victor Appleton
Victoria Cross
Virginia Woolf
Wadsworth Camp
Walter Camp
Walter Scott
Washington Irving
Wilbur Lawton
Wilkie Collins
Willa Cather
Willard F. Baker
William Dean Howells
William le Queux
W. Makepeace Thackeray
William W. Walter
William Shakespeare
Winston Churchill
Yei Theodora Ozaki
Yogi Ramacharaka
Young E. Allison
Zane Grey

*9 7 8 1 4 2 1 8 2 3 5 5 3 *